DREAMS

Science has taken the study of dreams out of the philosopher's den and located it firmly in the psychologist's laboratory. This fascinating book reveals some surprising results of tests on volunteer dreamers.

D0726952

DREAMS

Their Mysteries Revealed

by
Geoffrey A. Dudley
B.A. (Lond.)

THE AQUARIAN PRESS

First published 1969
Second Edition (completely revised, enlarged and reset) 1979

ISBN 0-85030-175-0

The Aquarian Press is part of the Thorsons Publishing Group, Wellingborough, Northamptonshire, NN8 2RQ, England

Printed in Great Britain by
Cox & Wyman Ltd, Reading, Berkshire

9 11 13 15 14 12 10 8

CONTENTS

CHAPTER ONE

MODERN SCIENCE AND ANCIENT BELIEFS

In recent years the study of dreams has received a fresh impetus from discoveries made in the psychological laboratory. From this new research has emerged a picture of dream life rather different from that which has traditionally held the field.

For centuries the human mind was considered to be the province of the philosopher. Speculations about its nature proceeded on metaphysical lines. What was true of psychology in general applied with equal force to that part of it which dealt with dreams. It was not until the advent of the experimental worker that psychology broke away from its parent discipline, and the light of scientific inquiry began to be focused on the mysterious world of sleep.

The older tradition is well represented by such philosophical approaches as that revealed in Cicero's *Somnium Scipionis*, which, enlightening as it must have been felt to be in its own day, can no longer be regarded as offering the acceptable insights demanded by modern man.

From the invention of the electro-encephalograph or brain-wave machine, as it is popularly called, arose the idea of examining the brain waves of patients while they slept. Accordingly subjects were asked to sleep in the psychological laboratory, where it was possible to take their EEGs. A study of the configurations of these brain waves occurring during sleep has led to some interesting conclusions about the nature of dreams and about their relation to sleep.

It has shown, for instance, that dreams occur

periodically during sleep at a regular interval of about an hour and a half between one burst of dream activity and the next. It has also shown that the duration of a dream can be as short as ten minutes or as long as half an hour. This is in striking contrast with the earlier beliefs that dreams last only momentarily and that a great deal of dream content can be compressed into a short space of time.

The advantage of this scientific attack on the problem of dream psychology has been that it permits a sleeping person to be awakened as soon as his brain waves show signs that he is dreaming. A much more reliable report can then be obtained of the dream which was passing through his mind at the instant of awakening. Dreamers have always been notorious for their inability to recollect what they were dreaming about, but with the application of science to this field the obstacle has now been overcome.

The pre-scientific belief that dreams are over in a very short space of time can be illustrated by the classic example reported by Maury, an earlier worker in this field. He dreamed that he was living at the time of the Reign of Terror during the French Revolution. He was about to be beheaded on the scaffold. As he felt the blade of the guillotine descend and cut off his head, he woke to find that part of his bed had collapsed and fallen on his neck. The traditional explanation is that the bed collapsed *before* the dream, which occurred in the brief interval between its striking his neck and the impact's waking him up. No matter how much credence was given to this explanation in the past, it is now no longer possible to accept it as true. The researches of Kleitman, carried on at the University of Chicago since 1952, have cast doubt upon its validity.

Kleitman centred his attention particularly on the eye movements made by persons while they slept. He arranged for these movements to be recorded along with the data provided by electro-encephalograph records of amplified electric currents given off by the brain. He found that rapid eye movements were accompanied by changes in the patterns of brain waves. When awakened, the sleeping persons in whom this had occurred reported that at that moment they had been dreaming. They usually failed to report any dreams if they were awakened during a period when there were no rapid eye movements. Kleitman concluded that these eye movements indicated the occurrence of a dream. Indeed, there seemed to be so close a correspondence between the two as to suggest that his sleeping subjects were following with their eyes the action depicted in their dreams.

For example, one subject reported a dream about two people throwing tomatoes at each other. His eyes were seen to be moving rapidly from side to side as though he were watching what was going on. Movements of the eyes in other directions also seemed to correspond with the kind of action which the subject reported as taking place in his dreams.

One piece of evidence from these laboratory studies has confirmed rather than refuted something that was previously thought to be true about dreams. This is the common belief that on waking in the morning we do not remember more than a fraction of the dreams which we have had during the night. The laboratory workers confirmed this belief when they noted that a subject who was left in the laboratory to sleep the whole night through without being disturbed was no better at recalling his dreams than is normally the case outside the laboratory.

Two other workers in this new field of scientific dream study are Shapiro and Goodenough. They compared two groups of New Yorkers. One group consisted of people who denied that they dreamed every night; the other consisted of people who said that they did. The sleep of both groups was monitored by means of the technique described above. No difference was found in the frequency of dreams reported by both groups. The conclusion is not, as used to be thought, that some people dream more than others, but rather that some people have better memories than others for their dreams.

The evidence suggests, in fact, that everyone dreams throughout the night at regular intervals. This is perhaps not surprising, seeing that we are all subjected to environmental pressures which block our natural impulses. It is from this element of 'repression', as Freud called it, that dreams take their starting-point.

Shapiro and Goodenough's study did, however, show that people who had previously failed to report dreams were more uncertain about whether or not they had actually been dreaming. 'I was asleep but thinking' was a common plea put forward by the members of the group who reported this experience.

To Dement, a colleague of Kleitman's, we owe the discovery that the brain-wave pattern associated with rapid eye movements resembles the pattern found when the subject is awake. This suggests that while they are dreaming the subjects' state of consciousness is more like that of waking life than that of non-dreaming periods during sleep.

Dement made three other discoveries which are of interest. These are:

1. Periods of brain activity are short at the beginning of the sleep period but increase in length as sleep progresses. We have seen above that these periods of brain activity coincide with the rapid eye movements and indicate the onset of a period of dreaming. This

means that our dreams are short ones soon after we have fallen asleep, but those which occur just before we wake up are longer.

2. During a period of eight hours' sleep this combined activity takes place at regular intervals of about an hour and a half. The first dream period, which lasts for about nine minutes, occurs about an hour after you have fallen asleep. The second, which lasts for about 19 minutes, occurs an hour and a half later. The third one, which lasts about 24 minutes, occurs an hour and a half after that. After a similar interval the fourth one comes along and this lasts about 28 minutes. There is another interval of an hour and a half before the fifth period, which lasts until it is interrupted by the sleeping person's return to consciousness.

3. The depth of sleep during the later periods of dreaming is less than that during the earlier ones. Are we entitled to infer that one of the functions of dreaming is to prepare the mind for waking up? At any rate this seems to be what is actually taking place during the mind's excursions into the realm of dreams.

Psychologists in Great Britain, too, have been working along these lines, and their researches have confirmed some of the findings of their American colleagues. For instance, at the University of Edinburgh, Oswald studied the eye movements of men who had suffered all their lives from blindness. It would be more accurate to say that he studied their lack of eye movements – for he found that they did not make any. It is well known that persons who have been blind from birth do not experience visual images in their dreams. Images are based on memories – and they have no memories of sight to go on. In showing that his congenitally blind subjects did not need to move their eyes because they were not looking at anything in their sleep, Oswald's results substantiated those of the American investigators who believed that eye movements reflected the dreamer's attention to what he was seeing in his dream.

We have indicated above that these studies have thrown doubt on the view that in dreams everything happens 'in a flash'. The brain-monitoring technique permits an accurate measurement of the time taken to dream a piece of action. This has been compared with the time required to perform the same action in reality. It has been found that there is no difference between the two. This dismisses the notion of the extreme rapidity with which events occur in dreams, for which support used to be claimed from such instances as the guillotine dream of Maury alluded to above.

We see, then, that under the impact of modern science some ancient beliefs about dreams fare better than others. Science has taken the study of dreams out of the philosopher's den and located it firmly in the psychological laboratory. Experimental work has called to its aid the electro-encephalograph. This has provided records which disclose periods of dream activity occurring at regular intervals and increasing in length throughout the total period of sleep. Such work has unseated the belief that in dreams everything happens in a flash, producing evidence that it takes as long to dream about something as actually to do it.

We find, too, that the depth of sleep decreases from beginning to end of the sleep period, and that the recurrence of dreams is detected by the sleeping person's rapid eye movements. These suggest that he is following with his eyes the actions which he is imagining while asleep. We now know, too, that we were right in thinking, as we always did, that we dream far more than we can normally remember in the morning.

CHAPTER TWO

NEW LIGHT ON YOUR SLEEP AND DREAMS

At least once a day, as a general rule, nature has provided for you to relinquish your hold upon reality and enjoy a period of deep, natural sleep. Life could not long endure constant functioning among the jangling discords and false thinking of the outer world. So once in every twenty-four hours you withdraw into the inner world of sleep to renew the physical energies impaired by the stress of your waking hours.

As we have seen in Chapter One, what happens when you fall asleep naturally has been established by a study of the patterns of the tiny electric currents given off by your brain during both sleep and wakefulness. The brain waves are amplified by the electro-encephalograph and can be recorded mechanically by pens which trace their patterns on rolls of paper. The movements of the eyes also produce electrical activity and this, too, can be recorded.

This research has shown that the process of sleeping can be divided into four stages. The first of these begins while you are still awake. While you are still conscious but preparing to go to sleep, the brain waves show an even pattern which denotes a state of relaxation and reduced thinking. This pattern can also be found in persons who during wakefulness fall into a 'brown study' or state of abstraction such as day-dreaming or meditation.

The second stage heralds the onset of true sleep. But at this stage you may suddenly return to consciousness with a 'jump'. The proper name for this 'jump' is a 'myoclonic spasm'. If you are suddenly awakened in this way, you may feel that you have not really been to sleep at all.

Once you are asleep, however, stage two is rapidly succeeded by stage three, in which the EEG records rapid bursts of brain activity. A person awakened even from this stage of sleep may still have the feeling that he has not really been to sleep.

In the fourth stage a slower pattern of brain waves emerges. There is a general slowing-down of bodily activities. The sleeping person's heart beats more slowly and his body temperature and blood pressure fall. You are sound asleep now.

This level of sleep is attained about half an hour after you have fallen asleep. It continues for about twenty minutes, when sleep begins to become less deep. You retrace your steps, as it were, back through the pattern of sleep which you have followed to reach the deepest level. You become progressively more and more 'awake', until after about ninety minutes you are back in stage two again.

This cycle of deep sleep alternating with light sleep continues throughout the night. During an average night's sleep there are four or five such alternating periods. As the night progresses, you spend gradually less and less time in stage four until eventually, of course, you end up by waking as morning approaches.

We have spoken of the sleep period as 'night', as this is usually the case, but what is described above also applies if you sleep during the daytime.

We also said that eye movements can be monitored during sleep. If this is done, the results show that slow eye movements occur during stages two, three, and four. As you reach stage one on the way back from stage four, your eye movements become rapid. These rapid eye movements are known as REMs.

Their significance is that you are experiencing vivid dreams, which can be recalled if you are then immediately awakened. During these periods, as we have noted, the eyes of the sleeping person are moving behind his closed lids as he watches the action of the events taking place in his dreams.

The dream that is remembered in the morning is usually the one which has occurred in the last period of dreaming before waking up. But we now know that we dream at intervals throughout the night. The other dreams are forgotten unless you are woken up immediately after they have occurred.

It has now been established that dreaming takes place not only during the REM periods but also during the periods of slower eye movements. However, there is a difference between the two types of dreams. REM dreams are vivid and prolonged; the others are less vivid and shorter. The latter are more like daytime thinking.

From what has been said so far the reader can see that we have now demolished two more popular fallacies about dreams. The first is that some people never dream. The evidence is that everyone dreams in the cyclic activity described above. The difference between people is not in how much they dream but in how well they remember their dreams.

Secondly, this newer knowledge of dream activity undermines the popular view that dreams are caused by indigestion. The truth is that we dream whether we have indigestion or not. But a disturbing stimulus arising from indigestion may be worked into the fabric of a dream that we are going to have anyway.

It used to be thought that insomnia is harmful because it deprives you of your sleep. It is now known that it is harmful because it deprives you of your dreams. Dreams seem to be essential to the health of the mind. Personality disturbances result if people are deprived of the opportunity to dream by being totally deprived of their sleep. We need our sleep, it is true, to restore our bodily resources, especially our brain tissues. But we also need our dreams to provide a fantasy outlet for our submerged psychological needs. This is a point of view which we shall be exploring more fully in Chapter Three.

We have mentioned two types of dreams – vivid ones occurring during REM periods and vague ones occurring at other points during the sleep cycle. There is yet a third kind, which usually occurs during stage one. It is the 'hypnagogic' dream or vision, which belongs to the shadowy borderland between wakefulness and sleep.

It is characterized by unusual physical sensations and strange hallucinations, which often take the form of faces or country scenes. A hypnagogic dream is often in colour, although this feature can be present in the two other types of dreams, especially the REM ones. This type of dream will be discussed further in Chapter Thirteen.

For most people, however, the main interest of the dream lies in the light which it throws on what is going on in the recesses of the dreamer's mind. If you are interested in dreams from this point of view, you can use both main types – vivid and vague – as a means of gaining insight into the inner workings of your psyche.

Let us take an actual example. In her book *Dream Power* (Hodder and Stoughton, 1972) Ann Faraday reports a dream of her own in which she was waiting at the rear entrance of Buckingham Palace for the Queen to arrive in her car from a visit to the Royal Marsden Hospital in Chelsea.

The dreamer comments on the usual interpretation of the Queen as a mother symbol, i.e., she represents the dreamer's own mother. In the word 'Marsden' she finds a pun on 'Ma's den', i.e., 'mother's house'. She discovers significance in the reference to the rear entrance, relating it to enemas she was given by her mother in childhood. She sees in the car a sex symbol in line with Freud's views on the role of symbols in dreams.

We can accept this analysis, which has already given the dreamer considerable insight into the meaning of her dream. We must criticize it, however, on the grounds that it does not go far enough: it does not deal with the major theme of the dream, which is *waiting*.

Waiting, in fact, is one of woman's major roles in life. *Waiting Women* is the literal translation of the Swedish title of one of Ingmar Bergman's films. Any of these films are worth seeing for the illuminating insights which they provide into the female mind. In them he shows how women *wait* for their lover to come, for their baby to be born, for their children to grow up. They *wait* for the menopause to free them from child-bearing; they *wait* for death to liberate them from life itself.

The dream, then, deals with an interesting difference between the sexes. It highlights the role of woman as the one who waits in contrast with the traditional role of the male, who is the one who makes things happen.

This dream hints at the possibility that the dreamer is attempting to reconcile herself to the female role in life. She is reassuring herself that if she waits, she will eventually be rewarded by the arrival of what is waited for. Perhaps, too, she is trying to convince herself that what is waited for is actually worth waiting for – that the ultimate realization which life provides will compensate her adequately for the period of limbo spent in waiting for it.

In many other dream actions besides waiting, you can seek a basic attitude of yours, as the dreamer, towards what the action symbolizes. And you can go on to tie up the dream symbol with its use outside dreams, e.g., in literature. For instance, if the motif of your dream is waiting, you might connect it with whatever meaning you can find in Samuel Beckett's play, in which Godot, who is waited for by two tramps, never arrives. What, you can ask yourself, is the playwright saying here that has an echo in the life of a woman who is waiting in her dream?

This simple example should encourage us to seek to broaden our insight. Our aim is to understand the significance of the inner life that springs into activity as we move up and down through the four stages of sleep in the way that modern research has now revealed to be a common feature of the dreams of all of us.

CHAPTER THREE

DO DREAMS KEEP US SANE?

In the previous chapters we saw how, by using the brain-wave machine, psychologists have been able to throw light on numerous problems of dream life. Another interesting finding which has emerged from these laboratory studies is this: subjects whose sleep was frequently interrupted in order to get them to report their dreams began to dream at more frequent intervals than the customary hour and a half.

It seems that dreams serve a necessary therapeutic function in releasing a person from the pressures of everyday life. If anything happens to interfere with this 'safety-valve', which perhaps guards our mental health, nature reasserts her beneficial influence on our behalf and insists that we will be compensated for what we have lost. She makes it possible for us to retreat oftener into the world of fantasy.

This may explain why insomnia is commonly believed to be harmful. The harm may come not so much from the fact that we are being deprived of our sleep as that we are being deprived of our opportunity to dream.

Some recent work in other fields has thrown further light on this discovery. Other workers have kept subjects under conditions of minimum stimulation. That is, they have paid volunteers twenty dollars a day to be confined in cubicles in circumstances which make it possible for them to touch, see, or hear very little. Few of them were able to endure more than 72 hours of this, in spite of the financial inducement. Subjects who persevered found that they began to develop hallucinations. The mind appears to create its own stimulation in the form of fantasies if normal channels of stimulation are cut off.

This may apply to the dreams of sleep, too. When we fall asleep, we are depriving ourselves of the stimulation afforded in waking life by our senses. The mind creates dreams to offset this deprivation. Dreams may well preserve the sanity which we might lose if our sleep were invariably dreamless.

It also appears to apply to the dreams which we have when we are not asleep, i.e., day-dreams. In a mine disaster in West Germany eleven colliers were trapped underground. It was two weeks before they could be brought to the surface by their rescuers. According to a medical report, their experiences of deprivation brought on hallucinations. 'One of them', says the report, 'wanted to dig a path to his home through the rock. Another tried to run through the walls. A particularly sensitive miner believed he was in a flowery meadow. He pretended to himself that he was picking cherries and spoke ceaselessly with his wife.'

What happened here is that the normal channels of stimulation from the outside world were cut off. Imprisoned in darkness without normal contact with the surface, these miners suffered conditions similar to those of the subjects in the laboratory experiment mentioned above, but for a very much longer time. Unable to endure the strain imposed by this understimulation, their minds created hallucinations to furnish a self-made source of stimulation. Although they were in pretty bad shape physically when rescued, they might have lost their sanity completely had not this mental safety-valve of day-dreams come to their aid during their terrifying ordeal.

The secret police in certain countries use this mechanism deliberately in 'brainwashing' their prisoners and extracting confessions from them. Prisoners of war have been brainwashed in the same way. By depriving the victims of sleep and mental stimulation, their captors break them down, obtain information from them, and plant ideas in their minds. Political prisoners are kept awake for hours on end during questioning by relays of interrogators. As this lack of sleep begins to exhaust the brain, the mind tends to hallucinate imaginary experiences. In addition, real experiences are introduced to the prisoner, like showing him obscene films, with the deliberate intention of confusing him and making it difficult for him to separate reality from fantasy. His loss of contact with the outside world and his anxiety about his future help to create additional sources of confusion, to which the mind responds with further fantasy-creation. The prisoner becomes suggestible and ready to accept ideas which are foreign to his usual way of thinking.

Eric Chou, a Chinese journalist, describes in *A Man Must Choose* (Longmans, 1963) how by this technique he was brought to a full and largely false confession during the four years he spent in communist jails.

Even in democratic countries, public concern has been expressed about police methods to a committee of High Court judges. Under English law a person cannot be detained in a police-station against his will unless charged with some offence, nor is he obliged to answer questions. Yet the mere fact of going to the police-station implies some loss of contact with his ordinary environment. Furthermore, repeated questioning by different police officials may induce some degree of fatigue, against which the mind begins to rebel. Confusion may set in: the suspect imagines things he has said and done; the mind creates these images by way of compensation for the strain occasioned by the circumstances. A person may unwittingly incriminate himself simply by confusing what has really happened with what his mind leads him to imagine under the pressure of being treated as a suspect.

'How often British police methods lead to false confessions', says a writer in the *Sunday Telegraph*, 'cannot be exactly known. But there have been quite a number of recorded instances.'

This compensatory role of fantasy as a means of relieving the pressure of reality is no doubt illustrated by the imaginative mental creativeness of poets, artists, writers, musicians, and so on. For example, Robert Louis Stevenson's wife once woke him in the small hours when he was uttering cries of horror. He reproached her for doing so, because, as he told her, he had been dreaming 'a mighty fine bogey tale'. It was later to become *The Strange Case of Dr Jekyll and Mr Hyde*. Warwick Deeping, too, wrote that he once dreamed a short story and got up at five in the morning to write it down. It is as though the mind needs the irrational element which is the mark of dreams as a way of offsetting our tendency during waking life to overwork the rational part of our nature.

Sometimes dreams deal directly with the need to stay sane or with the fear of losing our sanity. A young man who complained of a fear of going insane illustrates this point. He reported a dream in which he saw the devil. The devil represented the devilish desires within himself which he had repressed and for which, if he were insane, he would no longer be held responsible. His dream embodied a fear of his own nature combined with a wish to escape from himself into the insanity in which he would have been able to give free rein to all the impulses he had denied. He was using his dream life as an escape from the terrors that beset him in his waking life. He literally owed his sanity to his dreams.

It is interesting to observe that no reduction in the intervals between dreaming periods occurs if a laboratory subject is awakened regularly at times when the records of his brain activity and eye movements show that he is *not* dreaming. This means that although he is awakened and deprived of his sleep, he is not deprived of his opportunity to dream which sleep affords him. Consequently, he experiences no need to intensify his dreaming activity as a means of compensation, as he would if he were awakened at a time when he was actually dreaming.

Dement and his colleague Wolpert carried out an unusual experiment in which they squirted the faces of sleeping persons with a fine spray of water during one of the periods of dreaming. When awakened, the subject would report a dream into which the spray of water was introduced. For example, one subject dreamed that his roof was leaking and the rain was dripping in on him. However, no such dream was reported if the spray was used on the sleeping subject at times when his EEG record showed that he was not dreaming.

The relevance of this experiment is as follows: it used to be considered that any outside stimulus affecting a sleeping person would be worked into the fabric of his dreams. (Again we see an illustration of the function of the mind as an active seeker of stimuli.) The purpose of this was thought to be that the mind not only uses dreams to keep us sane, but it also attempts to preserve our sleep unbroken in the face of interruptions. For instance, if a person's bed-clothes have fallen off, he may dream that he is trudging through snowy wastes. As long as he continues to dream, he remains asleep, and so the stimulus of the cold does not deprive him of the benefits which sleep and the dreams accompanying it at regular intervals, confer.

However, it is now known that such an influence will have this effect not at *any* time during sleep but only at those times when a dream period is actually taking place. This is further proof that we sleep in order to dream, because we need the psychological advantages which dreams bring us in terms of preserving our mental health. The satisfaction of this need may be essential to the stability of the mind. A regular source of mental stimulation such as the nightly recurring dream cycle may be necessary to keep us from going insane.

Studies of the experiences of pilots of aircraft and long-distance lorry drivers tell the same story as those of brain-washed political prisoners and ordinary persons deprived of their sleep. For instance, solo pilots of high-altitude jet planes may develop a sense of being isolated from what is occurring on the ground. They may begin to have hallucinations, to hear voices, and to believe things that are not true, such as that they are not in a plane at all. Similar symptoms in a less intense form have been reported by lorry drivers who spend long hours of monotonous driving on high-speed motorways.

It seems that, deprived of stimulation, the mind will create its own, and it may well be that dreams, both those of sleep and day-dreams, help to keep the human mind on an even keel when loss of stimulation for one reason or another from the outside world threatens to throw it off balance. There is an important lesson that we have learned here about mental health, and it is one about which we should have remained largely ignorant had it not been for the newer scientific studies which have brought a flood of light to bear upon our mysterious inner selves.

CHAPTER FOUR

UNDERSTANDING OUR PROBLEMS

'I am a young man of seventeen', said Mr U. 'I have got myself emotionally involved with a friend who is fifteen. It all started three years ago. I have grown outstandingly fond of him. I do everything I can for him and give him all I can. I long to be with this friend all the time. I feel an urge to protect him. I feel that without him my life is finished. I have no feelings at all for the opposite sex.

'For the past eight years my parents have been unhappy together. My father told my mother that he was taking another woman out. She decided to leave him. He promised faithfully that he would leave the other woman alone, but recently my mother discovered that he is still hanging around this woman, who is married.'

This state of affairs did not have any noticeable effect on Mr U. until he discovered his friend Peter. His affection for this boy led him to feel that he should treat him as a father would treat a son. He tried to do this but found that sometimes he was violently repulsed. This made him so unhappy that he tried to commit suicide.

'I have an overwhelming desire', he continued, 'that Peter should come and live with us. At present he lives with his grandmother. She is planning to send him to a home, where I know he would be unhappy.'

He reported the following dream:

'Last night I dreamed that Peter was drunk and incapable. He was in hospital as a result of it. This made me feel guilty during the dream because I was not with him to look after him. When I woke I felt this sense of duty more strongly than ever. Can you please explain what has happened to me?'

Before we attempt to answer this question, it is worth
setting down in the mother's words how she saw the
same situation. It is not often that we are privileged to
look at the effects of an unhappy marriage from two
points of view. Later we shall see how discussion of this
problem, including analysis of the son's dream, helped
both mother and son to rise above their troubles.

'At the moment', said the mother, 'I am consulting a
solicitor with a view to obtaining either a divorce or a
separation. I cannot continue to live with my husband,
who has not the slightest interest in or concern for either
me or his son.

'My problem is: Am I going to do my son more harm
than good in taking him away with me? Is he likely to get
over his unhealthy attachment for this boy Peter, who is
not really particularly friendly with my son? One cannot
choose one's children's friends, and I have never tried in
any way to interfere.

'As far as Peter is concerned, I cannot believe for one
moment that his grandmother would turn him out of the
house. She does a lot of talking and nagging, but I am
sure it is all hot air. She has cared for Peter since her
daughter left her husband when Peter was quite small.

'As far as I am concerned, I feel I have enough on my
plate at the moment to find a home and a means of
earning my living without 'adopting' another problem
boy. However, I shall be most happy for Peter to spend
some week-end with us when we move away.'

The young man's dream provides a convenient key
with which to start to understand this problem. The
friend who is drunk and incapable symbolizes the
dreamer himself. This is why the dreamer does not
imagine himself being with his friend. He is there already
in the guise of the friend.

The dream expresses his wish to be looked after as a
means of compensating himself for his sense of

insecurity. In waking life this wish to be looked after has been translated into a wish to look after someone else in whom he can see his own problem.

In the dream Mr U. feels guilty because he realizes that his wish to be looked after conflicts with what is normally expected of an adult person. Responsible adults are expected to look after the less responsible members of society. This is, in fact, what the dreamer is trying to do in waking life. The dream shows that he is doing it in an attempt to relieve himself of the feelings of guilt provoked by his own wish to be looked after.

Mr U.'s affection for Peter has led him to feel that he should treat him as a father would treat a son. It is clear that he himself is striving to be the loving father that he has failed to find in his own father. He wants to treat Peter as he would have liked his father to treat him. He identifies himself with a father figure in order to compensate himself for the lack of fatherly guidance in his own life.

As emotional maturity approaches, the teenager tends to become less interested in himself and more interested in others. But if he focuses his interest only on his own sex, he is treading dangerous ground. A certain amount of homosexual response is normal in all of us. We find some friends of our own sex more attractive socially than others. But we should not spend our waking hours seeking out the company of someone who fits our preconceived notions of such a partnership.

Although it doesn't appear in his dream, another factor probably enters into Mr U.'s problem. The failure of his relationship with his father may have intensified his devotion to his mother. He may, in fact, be overattached to her, so that he avoids girls out of a sense of loyalty. He believes that they might lead him to be unfaithful to his mother. As he himself put it: 'I am all my mother has.' It would not be surprising if he were to report a dream in which this theme appears in disguised form.

It was not long before discussing the problem with son and mother began to show results in the lives of both. They decided to move away from the father, and found themselves a cottage at an inexpensive rent.

'I have new confidence in myself', reported Mr U. 'I now feel that I have a right to enjoy life as much as anyone else. I did not expect results quite so quickly, but the interpretation of my dream proved particularly illuminating. My father now has a much better attitude towards me. I can lead a normal life. It is like waking from a deep and endless sleep. I can make decisions more freely and the shadow of doubt is leaving me. I feel as if I have at last severed the chains which threatened to hold me back from peace and happiness. I find myself taking a new interest in people.'

He added that he now realized just who he was and no longer thought of himself as an outcast. He was beginning to realize his good points and to take advantage of them. Lots of people had remarked on his improvement.

'I can now look upon Peter as a normal friend,' he continued, 'and when I visited him last week-end, I was struck by the change in my attitude towards him.

'I am now in a job that I really enjoy. This is of paramount importance to me. All my feelings of inferiority are being wiped out and are being replaced by a self-assurance which nothing can shake.

'I am certainly living a fuller and more confident life. I find people friendlier towards me. I have risen above that sordid homosexual state into a more socially acceptable way of living. I am taking more and more interest in girls.

'I hope that understanding their dreams and gaining insight into their motives will encourage other people who are as unfortunate as I once was.'

Of his mother Mr U. said: 'She is looking younger. All the lines and wrinkles are dropping from her face, and she is a much happier person.'

A significant remark made by the son was: 'My father now has a much better attitude towards me.' It illustrates something that we need no dream interpretation to tell us. This is that we command no one's respect when we meekly accept a degrading situation. When we begin to take some active step to deal with it, people begin to look up to us more. Our positive action deserves and receives the respect of those who previously were inclined to pity and despise us for our indecision.

The moral of this real-life story is that teenagers are people with normal hopes and fears. These are reflected in their dreams as our own are in the dreams of all of us. If we can learn to read the messages that thus come to us in our sleep, this learning experience can release our normal capacities for happiness. The destructive effect of an unhappy home life upon adolescent character is powerfully illustrated by this situation. We may feel a sense of profound gratitude that dream interpretation contributed in no small measure to its satisfactory outcome.

CHAPTER FIVE

TEN TYPICAL DREAMS

No dreams are utter nonsense, although they often seem to be. All can be interpreted if the key to the meaning can be found. In order to interpret a dream fully, it is desirable to have the dreamer's 'associations' to it. These are the thoughts and memories of which the dream reminds him. If he pursues them closely enough, he is likely to discover in them a clue to the correct interpretation. This method reveals the unconscious mental conflicts and wishes which form the psychological basis of the dream. It is for this reason that Freud called dreams 'the royal road to the unconscious'.

Nevertheless, there are certain dreams which can often be understood without benefit of the dreamer's associations. This is because such dreams are widespread throughout the human race and have a universal meaning relating to the basic problems of life and death which concern all dreamers. Such dreams are called 'typical' dreams and in this chapter we describe ten of them.

1. *Missing a train.* This typical dream occurs with great frequency. According to psycho-analysis, it refers to a journey that everyone is compelled to make: the journey through life to the grave. A person who has died is spoken of as 'the departed', as though he had gone on a journey. This dream reflects the dreamer's unconscious wish to reassure himself against the fear of death. By missing the train he says to himself: 'I shall not die'.

On the other hand, Adler's school of Individual Psychology ascribes a different meaning to the dream. 'Dreams of failure to catch a train', writes Lewis Way in

Adler's Place in Psychology, 'may in general denote a fear of being left behind in the race for life or may indicate a wish to arrive too late to solve the problem.'

Probably both interpretations are to be accepted as true, the real question being that of their relative importance in any particular case.

The fundamental idea in this dream is that of taking a journey, and the means of transportation is not always a train. Some dreamers 'miss the bus' instead. This, however, does not affect the interpretation. The wish is always to avoid taking the journey, i.e., not to die.

2. *Looking for a room.* This dream is common in the experience of women. If the dreamer is a single woman, it usually relates to her wish to get married. For example, a young girl dreamed: 'I am looking over a house; wandering through all the rooms.' The close connection between the ideas of going over the house and being married is seen in the word 'housewife'. The dream reflects the thought: 'I want to find my own house. I want to become a housewife.' Dining-room and bedroom combine the two elements of 'bed and board', which constitute marriage from a purely material point of view. If the dreamer is looking through several rooms, this conveys the idea of monogamy by the law of opposites which often plays a prominent part in dreams.

In married women the meaning is rather different. A married woman dreamed: 'I am staying in an hotel with a lot of bedrooms and can never find my own. I seem to spend hours going up and down stairs and get very weary, but I have never yet found the correct room.' In *The Interpretation of Dreams* Freud says that a room is used to symbolize a woman. In looking for her room in an hotel the dreamer is looking for another woman, i.e., her other self. The dream reflects a desire to find her true self (the correct room).

3. *Climbing.* A dreamer said that nearly all his dreams

were connected with climbing. He added that he never seemed to reach the top until one night he had a dream in which he achieved this. 'The joy I felt in my sleep', he said, 'was just indescribable.'

He quoted four lines of a poem which he had learned during his school-days and had never forgotten. They were:

> The heights that great men reached and kept
> Were not attained in sudden flight,
> But they while their companions slept
> Were toiling upwards in the night.

The fact that the content of the poem is the same as the content of his dreams is significant. Obviously climbing is important to him. The symbolic meaning which the poem gives to this activity is the meaning which should be given to it in the dream. That is, climbing signifies achieving an ambition. When he dreamed that he had reached the top, it looks as though his confidence in his ability to achieve his ambition had reached its peak.

4. *Falling*. Climbing may also have a sexual significance especially when associated with falling. It may then symbolize the rise and fall of sexual excitement. For example, a lady once asked me about the meaning of the stereotyped dream which she had been having for several years: 'I am climbing a mountain under great difficulty. When I am almost at the top, I suddenly lose my balance and start to fall.'

This dream expressed the dreamer's sexual frigidity. Here the top of the mountain symbolizes the climax of sexual sensation. This she was unable to achieve in her marital life. She attempted in her dream to gratify the wish to achieve it, but was not quite successful in doing so.

'Falling' has an emotional significance even in everyday speech. We talk of falling into temptation, of falling from grace, of falling in love, and so on. This applies equally to dreams, in which the literal act of falling symbolizes the figurative one.

5. *Flying and floating on air.* The person who dreams that he is flying may suffer from an inferiority complex, for which he is compensating himself by showing other people how clever he is. For example, a man said: 'I can remember one dream that is always outstanding: a dream of flying over people's heads, in which I am shouting to them to take notice of me.'

The dream may also relate to the wish to triumph over difficulties in general. For example, a man of sixty said: 'I bought my own business and found I had bought a load of worry, trouble, financial difficulties, and very hard work. During all this time I used to have a dream in which I was flying or floating through the air with the ease of a bird. It was a lovely sensation and I used to enjoy it immensely. About the time when I sold the business I had my last flying dream.'

When this man had his dreams of flying, he was trying to surmount the difficulties arising from his business deal. In his dreams he was saying to himself: 'I can rise above all my troubles.' When he sold the business, he ceased to have the flying dream. This was because, having got rid of the source of his worry, he no longer needed to assure himself in his dreams that he could surmount his difficulties.

6. *Running from a pursuer.* A 23-year-old schoolteacher dreamed that she was being chased by someone. 'I remember running hard', she said, 'and being very much afraid, but at the same time I remember looking back and trying desperately to see who or what was chasing me.'

Dreams of being chased, when they occur in young single women, symbolically gratify the wish to be wooed by a lover. They contain a pun on the word 'chased' (chaste), so that the wish is to be wooed without losing one's virginity.

This is made explicit by another woman, who described the following nightmare: 'I am running for my life, as I am being chased by a man. I always seem to manage to escape. Sometimes someone gives me shelter and hides me until the danger is past. There is almost always a middle-aged woman there, and to everyone else she is a respectable woman, but she hates me and is an accomplice.'

The dreamer's associations to this dream of pursuit contain the meaning. They were: 'My interpretation concerns courtship days. My natural wish was to be happily married, but when I went out with a boy-friend, I was very wary of his intentions. My husband and I had a tiff about this during our engagement. The middle-aged woman may be my mother, who advised me to be careful when out with boys.'

7. *Crime and punishment.* Mrs R.K. reported two interesting dreams. One was seeing one or other of her parents die. The other was of being in court.

Psychologically a 'crime' is a thought or wish of which the dreamer's conscience disapproves. Hostile thoughts or wishes against a parent are gratified by imagining that parent's death. This is the explanation of the first dream.

This gratification, however, cannot be achieved without the dreamer's feeling guilty about it. The sense of guilt makes her feel that she deserves to be punished. The need of punishment is satisfied by her imagining herself being brought up in court.

The two dreams belong psychologically together. The one depicts the punishment intended to atone for the sense of guilt arising from the 'crime' depicted in the other. Of course, such pairs of dreams don't always occur together, or at least both dreams are not always remembered. Sometimes only one is recalled, the memory of the other being repressed or disowned because to the dreamer's conscience it is too terrible to contemplate.

8. *Taking an examination*. A young teacher, who was awaiting the results of an examination he had taken, dreamed that he had received a telegram telling him that he had passed. It is not difficult to detect the wish-fulfilment in this typical dream. Such a dream may also relate to some 'examination' in the school of life, i.e., some trial or testing experience which the dreamer is anxious to pass with flying colours.

Can an examination dream be predictive? This, too, seems to be possible. For example, Miss T.E. said: 'About five years ago I was preparing for an exam. On the night before the exam I dreamed that I saw the examiner. I had never seen him before and I was sitting writing the exam. The next morning the man at the desk turned out to be exactly the same man whom I had seen in my dream. What is more, I found myself seated at exactly the same place in the examination hall that I had dreamed about.'

9. *Death and dying*. An elderly lady very vividly remembered twice dreaming that she was dead. Once she found herself in a large judgment hall in a cave, and in the second dream she was radiantly happy living in a very lovely country.

This dream illustrates the fact that a person cannot dream that he does not exist. Even if he dreams that he is dead, he still manages to survive as a spectator of his own death.

The dream-thought 'I wish I were dead', which is gratified by such dreams, means 'I wish I had not been born.' The wish is for the blissful pre-birth life in the mother's womb, which is symbolized by the large cave. In dreams, rounded or hollow objects like caves are regularly used by the unconscious mind as symbols of the maternal womb.

It is from this blissful state of life before birth that we derive our ideas of immortality, i.e., of a blissful existence after death. Such an existence may be symbolized, as here, by a lovely country where all the inhabitants are radiantly happy. This symbolism can be found not only in dreams but also in poetry, religion, mythology, spiritualism, art, and so on.

If we dream of the death of others, it means that unconsciously we want to get rid of them. For example, Freud was once told about a man who dreamed regularly about the death of his children. Freud surmised that the man was unhappily married and regarded the existence of the children as an obstacle to a divorce. The interpretation turned out to be correct, since the man was maintaining a relationship with his secretary.

10. *Appearing naked in public.* 'I am walking down the street', said a dreamer, 'and I suddenly realize that I am inadequately clothed. I feel terrible shame and embarrassment, and yet cannot get out of the crowd.' Dreams of this type are very common. The dreamer herself reported that two friends of hers had told her that they had both had the same dream.

The dream of being naked or inadequately clothed may mean that the dreamer would like to expose to other people that aspect of her personality which she regards as her true self. The dream reflects a wish on the part of the dreamer to let others see her as she really is. The embarrassment may reflect a fear of the disapproval of others if the dreamer dares to be herself. A metaphorical exposure of this kind is symbolized by a literal one, as is also done in ordinary speech in such expressions as 'the naked truth', 'baring one's soul', etc.

These ten types of dream do not exhaust the list of possible 'typical' dreams, but at least they illustrate the versatility of the dream mind. The fact that such dreams are so common also shows that under the skin people are very much alike. These dreams occur frequently among large numbers of people because they deal with the general similarities among people: the emotions that all share in common. For this reason they are worthy of study for the light which they shed on the hidden recesses of human nature.

CHAPTER SIX

TWO DREAMS: ONE MEANING

A South African man reported the two dreams that follow:

1. 'I was at a railway station waiting for a train to take me to some unknown destination. As I stood on the platform, I saw a locomotive coming in at full speed. I thought it was being driven recklessly. It overturned and the rails were torn from the sleepers.'

2. 'I stood on a railway platform waiting for a train. I noticed some lovely young women around. I looked towards the waiting-room and saw a naked woman and a Chinese standing there talking to each other. I felt embarrassed. When I looked at her again, she had grown incredibly large. I could not believe my eyes.'

Two dreams reported by the same dreamer enable us to take advantage of the principle that a dream can be interpreted with the aid of another dream. This is especially true if both dreams occur on the same night. We often find that what is shown disguised in one dream is shown openly in the other. Let us see how this principle applies to the two dreams described above.

For this purpose we should start first with the second dream, the meaning of which seems the more obvious of the two. Here the sexual wish is expressed openly. The dream reveals without disguise the dreamer's own sexual desires, about which he feels embarrassed.

It is possible that this dream revives a dim memory of some repressed sexual incident of his childhood. This is probably the significance of the increase in size of the naked woman. To a child the things and people of the adult world appear incredibly large, and it is this impression which is reflected in the dream.

Having detected the wish which this second dream gratifies openly, we must now look for a symbolic gratification of the same wish in the first dream. This is, in fact, what we do find. There are certain male sexual symbols in this dream. They are the locomotive, the rails, and the sleepers.

There is in both dreams a discordant element hinting at the possibility of disaster. This factor embodies the reaction of the dreamer's conscience to the open or symbolic expression of the sexual wish. In the second dream the wish is treated as something foreign to the dreamer's personality. This is symbolized by the presence of the Chinese. In the first dream it is symbolized by the overturning of the locomotive.

Here are examples of two more dreams, each of which throws light on the other. One of them, interestingly enough, also contains the railway-station motif. They were experienced by a married man of thirty-five:

1. 'I went to a small country railway station. There was no platform or train but only a long waiting-room without windows. I saw a woman who resembled my mother.'

2. 'My grandmother was riding a motor cycle. I was seated on the pillion.'

The dreamer's mother appears undisguised in the first dream, which deals with dying. Death is symbolized as a rail journey, for which the dreamer goes to the station. The absence of a platform and a train reassures him that he will not take the journey (will not die). This piece of symbolism was explained in the previous chapter. The dream shows that dying is identified with returning to the womb, which is represented by the long, windowless waiting-room. (In the womb the infant waits to be born.) While the person of the mother appears as the woman resembling the dreamer's mother, the reassurance against the fear of dying is disguised as avoiding the taking of a journey.

In the second dream, however, the journey is more clearly indicated, but for 'grandmother' the first dream tells us that we must read 'mother'. The dreamer's dependence upon his mother is openly shown by his riding behind her on the journey that they are taking together.

We have here, then, a further illustration of the fact that two dreams by the same dreamer may express the same wish in different forms, and for this reason can be used to interpret each other. The dream-monitoring technique described earlier has also confirmed that two dreams of a single dreamer may have one or more common elements or may toy with different solutions of the same problem.

Here is a case in which the point is illustrated by *three* dreams of the same dreamer. Each of these dreams deals with the infantile fantasy already alluded to, i.e., that of returning to the womb. The dreams were as follows:

1. 'I undressed at a bathing pool, came out on to the balcony, and jumped from there straight into the pool, which proved to be empty. I immediately got up, said, "That's enough of that", and went and dressed.'

2. 'I ran down some steps which led to a pond and dived straight into the pond. The water was very shallow and had a horrible taste. I tried to get out of it as quickly as I could. Several people sitting round the pond started laughing.'

3. 'I again jumped into a swimming pool and again it was very shallow and the water had a horrible taste.'

These three dreams are really only one dream with variations. The basic motif is the idea of diving into water. In the language of the unconscious mind this symbolizes returning to the womb, where the first nine months of life are actually spent surrounded by water, i.e., the amniotic fluid.

The dreams, however, bring out the futility of the dreamer's wish and subject it to ridicule. This is the adult side of himself disapproving of his infantile self. After jumping into the pool he found that it was empty. The people sitting round the pond started laughing. The water had a horrible taste. Each dream in its own way expresses the same thought. All these different features embody one idea: the dreamer's own opinion that a wish to return to the life before birth is futile, ridiculous, and unpleasant.

Two dreams on the same night often stand in a cause-and-effect relation to each other. This is illustrated by a dream in two parts (really two dreams) described by an Air Force officer. The two-part dream was experienced by a woman friend of his. 'She is also friendly', he said, 'with a brother officer and sometimes goes out with him.'

The woman dreamed that she was sitting with the first officer beneath a big tree with spreading roots. A small stream was running nearby. They were talking and the dreamer was feeling very happy. 'Then the scene changes', she went on, 'and I was alone in a strange room with only one door. Someone was trying to get in and I was using all my strength to keep him out. I started screaming and from somewhere I heard Mummy's voice saying, "Hold on, Andrew is coming!" Then I saw you.'

The first officer added: 'Although my friend knew me for a long time, we did not really take to each other until two years after the other chap had started going out with her. She has told him that she could not go out with him very often, but he keeps on pestering her all the same.'

The first half of the dream represents the lady's wish to be in the company of the officer who related the dream. This is the effect. The second half of the dream reveals the cause. She wants to be with him because she believes that he can rescue her from some danger that threatens her. The would-be intruder is no doubt the other officer. He represents the danger from which the dreamer wishes to be protected by her first officer friend.

'I would like to tell you about certain dreams which you may be able to help me to understand', said Miss R.E., a teacher. 'All of them I have had on at least several occasions.'

The dreams she reported were as follows:

1. 'I am going along a road but making very slow progress, because I am walking on my knees. I seemed to regard this laborious method as conventional.'

2. 'I dream of waking up tired with my eyelids stuck together. I cannot get them open no matter how hard I try.'

3. 'I am out in my night-clothes walking about the streets.'

She added that in all three dreams there was an overwhelming sense of frustration.

These three are really one dream in that they all have the same theme. The theme is based upon a conflict between the wish to do something and a sense of frustration at being unable to. Thus, in the 'road' dream the dreamer wishes to make progress but is frustrated by her method of walking. In the second dream she wishes to wake up but is frustrated by being unable to open her eyes. In the third dream she is frustrated by being inadequately dressed. (The wish does not appear in this dream, but we can assume that it is the wish to be accepted as she is.)

If this dreamer were to examine her waking experiences, she might well conclude that the conflict expressed in her dreams is characteristic of her life in general. She is probably reviving the conflict under various guises in her dreams in order to give herself an opportunity of getting to grips with it, of accustoming herself to it, or of exploring the possibility of doing something to solve it.

Having discussed and illustrated the point that two or more dreams may have the same meaning, let us conclude by asking: Can a single dream have more than one interpretation? The answer to this question is: Yes, since the way you interpret dreams depends to some extent upon the theoretical premises to which you subscribe. Dr J.A. Hadfield illustrates this in his *Dreams and Nightmares*, in which he interprets a dream in no less than four ways in accordance with his own views and those of Freud, Adler, and Jung.

The dream was: 'I was staying in a country house, and after everyone had gone to bed, I went downstairs to get the coal that was left on the sitting-room fire to take to my own bedroom. When I had taken the fire and reached the passage outside, I was met by a primitive Negro who threatened me. I tackled him and got him down, but then did not know what to do next. Then came a female form and said, "Don't kill or hurt him, but send him to a reformatory".'

The various interpretations he suggests are:

1. *Hadfield:* The dreamer's rebellion against society (stealing the fire) aroused primitive instincts (the Negro) which he had difficulty in repressing. His intuition (the female form) says, 'Don't destroy or repress them but reform them.'

2. *Freud:* The Negro represents the dreamer's father and the female form his mother. The defeat of the Negro fulfils the wish to get rid of the father in order to possess the mother (Oedipus complex). The remark about reforming the Negro instead of killing or hurting him is a concession to the dreamer's guilt feelings.

3. *Adler:* The dream depicts the urge to power, the dominance of the masculine urge as against the inferior feminine role; or it points to the trouble that results from lack of co-operation (stealing the fire).

4. *Jung:* The dream resembles the myth of Prometheus, who stole fire from the gods. The Negro represents the dark, troublesome forces of the racial unconscious. The female form is the feminine function in the dreamer's personality, to which he should pay heed in order to compensate for those powerful forces.

It would be a mistake to suppose that one of these interpretations is right and the others wrong. We would prefer to think that they are all true in the sense that each one presents a different aspect of the truth. For if the dream mind is as complex as we believe it is, a dream ought to be capable of more than one interpretation.

As Dr Emil A. Gutheil writes in his *Handbook of Dream Analysis*, 'Because several experiences may be condensed into one dream picture, we sometimes have to put several cross-sections through a dream. We find single details in dreams to be foci of several intersecting lines of thoughts and ideas. That is the reason why, when reconstructing thoughts and ideas, we often get more than one interpretation for a dream.'

This being so, it is not difficult for us to accept the fact that several dreams may be based upon one experience. For this reason, as we have seen, they may be capable of being given a single meaning.

CHAPTER SEVEN

MACABRE DREAMS OF MURDER

'It is very probable', writes Freud in his *Introductory Lectures on Psycho-Analysis*, 'that the dreamer knows something about his dream; the problem is how to make it possible for him to get at his knowledge and impart it to us. We do not expect him immediately to tell us what his dream means, but we do think he will be able to discover its sources, from what circle of thoughts and interests it is derived ...

'When the dreamer declares that he has no ideas, we shall contradict him, press him to answer, assure him that he must have some idea ... When I ask a man to say what comes to his mind about any given element in a dream, I require him to give himself up to the process of free association which follows when he keeps in mind the original idea.'

This means that you yourself can interpret one of your own dreams since it is your own mental product. You can do it by using the dream as the starting-point for a series of free associations on the lines described in Chapter Five. How this works out in practice is illustrated by the experience of Mr P.H.A.; who described the following macabre dream:

'I found myself standing over a dead body, which had every appearance of strangulation by hand. The corpse was that of an old woman who was totally unknown to me. The sickening feelings of fear and revulsion were so intense that words fail to do them justice.

'I have vague memories of carrying the dead body into a large, damp vault, where I prised up a flagstone, dug a grave beneath, and concealed the cadaver. I then took infinite pains to see that everything was left as it had been before.

'The macabre episode continued with an investigation, in which I suffered the tortures ascribed to the damned, believing that at any moment my grim secret would be discovered.

'Then the whole dream lost all semblance of coherent action and dissolved into a muddle of dingy coffins and obscene bones. Last of all there was a grave which was slowly subsiding in the middle, its headstone reeling drunkenly over the point of subsidence.'

The dreamer added: 'It still makes me shudder when I think of it. I am not of a vicious turn of mind nor do I have sanguinary inclinations of any kind. I sincerely hope you will not think I am attempting to put over fiction, although I must admit the whole thing suggests that. I would be grateful for your reading of this dream, while hoping that it will not reveal in me some hideous streak of which I have been ignorant. I cannot account for it; my mental condition was sound enough by average standards; I had not been reading weird fiction. And certainly I can think of nothing in the past that could be even remotely connected with it ... except, possibly, that the vault was rather like one which I had seen years before beneath the ruins of an old nunnery.'

Here we have the disclaimer referred to by Freud – the dreamer's denial of all knowledge of the associated circumstances of his dream apart from one small detail. So we do what Freud advises us to do: we press him to answer. He was advised to start by thinking of 'an old woman' and then go on to write down his thoughts and memories just as they came to him without any attempt to censor them. In this way, we assured him, it should be possible for him to convince himself that he knows who the old woman is and why he harbours death wishes against her.

In general, dreams in which murder is committed are not all that uncommon. They illustrate a remark that Freud makes in *The Interpretation of Dreams* to the effect that all dreams, including apparently guileless ones, show 'the mark of the beast'. For example, a 43-year-old Lancashire housewife dreamed that she killed a man who was trying to steal a key. 'I battered him with a shovel', she said. 'There was blood all over.'

The dreamer's associations to this dream were that she worried because her husband preferred drinking with other men to taking her out. He had a fairly well-to-do material position although, since he kept her short of money, this was not of much advantage to her.

The man who is killed in the dream is presumably her husband, who she believes holds the key to her happiness. She has reason to harbour aggressive thoughts against him since she has complained that he neglects her. This dream apparently provided a much-needed safety-valve for the dreamer's hostility against her husband.

Another man had dreams of committing murder. These he described in much the same way as Mr P.H.A. It was obvious that he had aggressive and sadistic wishes that found an outlet in his dreams, which also threw light on his choice of a career. He was a professional boxer. This activity provided an outlet in waking life for the wishes that appeared in his dreams. It enabled him to inflict pain and indulge in brutality in a socially acceptable way.

But to return to Mr P.H.A., who reported that his efforts to conduct an inquiry into the origin of his dream had 'met with an immediate and unqualified success'. The singling-out of the term 'old woman' had been enough to enable him to construct an entire line of thought that led to the correct interpretation.

'When I left school', he said, 'I was apprenticed to the

shoemaking trade in a small non-union factory employing some twenty men and women. My employer was a fine man who had worked hard with little success. Eventually this was changed by an increase in government contracts, which led to an expansion of his business and premises. He now grew petty, petulant, arrogant, pompous, avaricious, and harsh, losing the esteem of his employees. On account of his cantankerous and edgy nature, he was often referred to as "an old woman".

'Unfair piece-rates of pay which he devised upset the workmen badly. Although there was much grumbling, they hadn't the nerve to take it up with the boss himself. I had to be their scapegoat, being a young fool filled with impassioned ideals and the desire to beat a big drum in a good cause. I was sent to tackle the lion in his den.

'As you know, a man of mature years finds little difficulty in humiliating a lad of nineteen. He fell upon me with every wicked aspersion that he could conjure from an overwrought and keenly imaginative mind. I was a young blackguard, a menace to civilized society, an agitator, a threat to the development of the firm. He sacked me on the spot and threatened to make it impossible for me to get any other job in the locality.

'For being stupid enough to fight the battles of men three times my age I deserved a measure of punishment, but I think I hardly deserved the confidence-destroying treatment which was meted out to me. I was in a state of saddened bewilderment at the loathsome employer that I had once admired and respected. He is the only man for whom I have ever felt extreme hatred. To this day I detest him with unabated venom.

'So I think the reading of the dream runs like this. The "old woman" was the boss. The burial of the corpse represented my desire that the untruths that had been spoken about me should not be communicated to other people who had the power to do me harm. The agony I suffered during the investigation was that which afflicted me when my character was torn to shreds. The final chaos was the subjective manifestation of a broken life, the very tombstone falling on me in contempt.'

We must agree that Mr P.H.A.'s interpretation of his own dream is undoubtedly true. It illustrates the following points:

1. A dream figure who appears to be unknown to the dreamer may really be someone who is known very well to him and who has, in fact, been of considerable emotional significance to him.

2. A female figure in a dream may represent someone of the opposite sex. A chance association that uncovers this may be evoked in the course of the dreamer's analysis of his own mental product. Mr P.H.A.'s interpretation suggests the possibility that a masculine type of woman might appear in a dream in the guise of a man. We have known this to be reported by dreamers too.

3. The dream mind represents a wish by the act that corresponds to it, since the two are unconsciously identified with each other. Thus the hostile death wish against the employer is gratified by the dream, which depicts his death as an accomplished fact.

4. The dreamer can interpret his own dream by applying to it the method of free association. This yields the latent dream thoughts containing the wish-content of the dream.

5. The dream and the associations illustrate the ambivalence of emotions that characterizes the unconscious mind. The 'good' employer who was once admired and respected turned into a feared and hated object when he became the 'bad' slave-driver. In spite of the thoughts of intense hatred vented upon the victim, the admiration and respect still survive in the sense of

guilt and remorse which attended the murder and disposal of the body.

This dreamer associated dreams with occultism and esoteric doctrines. 'It is my honest belief', he affirmed, 'that there are forces at the very Well of Life which have devastating power over individual destinies, group destinies even.' Certainly his dream illustrates this. Good and evil are often so closely allied that only specialized knowledge can discern the difference between them. Dream interpretation, by drawing upon our inner resources, is part of a striving towards the paths of Light and the fundamental good of mankind.

CHAPTER EIGHT

CRIME AND PUNISHMENT

Of particular interest for the light which they shed upon each other are pairs of dreams of the type known as 'crime and punishment' dreams. These were referred to briefly in Chapter Five. In each pair of dreams of this type one dream depicts the punishment for the 'crime' portrayed in the other. A 'crime', as we have seen, is to be understood in the sense of some thought, wish, or memory of which the dreamer's conscience disapproves. The commission of the 'crime' in one dream gives rise to feelings of guilt which are atoned for by means of the self-inflicted punishment imagined in the other dream.

Here is a pair of dreams which illustrate this point:

1. 'I was involved quite accidentally in a swindle. I was terribly upset about it and was trying to explain the circumstances to someone in a darkened room. Suddenly I realized that in a corner of the room a third person was listening. I did not see the face either of the person to whom I was speaking or of the person listening.'

This is the 'crime' dream, the crime being represented by the swindle in which the dreamer is trying to explain her involvement. The actual crime of which she was accusing herself could be ascertained from a study of her waking life. She felt guilty about having separated from her husband and having put an end to her marriage by divorce. In the dream she is trying to justify this action, because she is anxious that no one should think badly of her.

In dreams people whose faces cannot be seen usually represent some aspect of the dreamer's own personality. This implies that the dreamer is trying to explain to herself what had happened in her married life. The darkened room symbolizes the mental obscurity surrounding the 'swindle' that her marriage had turned out to be. The hidden person who is listening in a corner of the room probably represents her own conscience.

2. 'I was a captive of a group of people who were taking me to a place of execution. Passing a shed, I noticed a cow which had been suspended by its legs from the ceiling. I remembered thinking that if these people could be so cruel to an animal, I could expect no mercy from them for myself.'

This second dream embodies the punishment for the crime depicted in the first one. In the second dream the dreamer is being taken to a place of execution where she will be strung up like a cow. She is really sitting in harsh judgment on herself, treating herself as a 'cow'; her punishment for the 'crime' which she has committed is no less than that she deserves to die.

A further study of this dreamer's waking life also disclosed that she suffered from blushing. We can assume that this habit, too, expressed the same feelings of guilt which were reflected in her dreams. It implied that the emotional forces which disrupted her marriage were still with her – in the form of this and other nervous symptoms with which she was afflicted.

Another woman dreamed:

'My son had been sentenced to death. I don't remember what his crime was. He wasn't kept in prison but was allowed to stay at home until his execution. As I didn't know when this was to be, I was afraid every time he went out in case he didn't return. One night he went out and left his dance programme behind. Instead of the word "Interval" the programme said "Hanging", and I knew then that I should never see him again. I was in a terrible state and had to have sedatives to calm myself down.'

This is a punishment dream. Although the 'crime' is referred to, the actual nature of it is suppressed. But we can arrive at it by means of analysis. A son's 'crime', according to psycho-analysis, is simply that he loves his mother, i.e., he is his father's rival. This is the well-known Oedipus complex named after the ancient Greek myth of Oedipus, who unwittingly slew his father and married his mother. When Oedipus learned about his crime, he punished himself by putting out his own eyes.

It is possible that the dreamer feels that the son has come between herself and her husband. This may be the 'crime' for which she feels that he deserves to hang. The dream shows, however, that she is trying to convince herself that the situation is not quite so serious as she imagines it to be. Thus, although her son is to be executed, he is allowed his freedom to live at home and even attend dances.

The son's living at home also gratifies a wish on the dreamer's part. It looks as though she is emotionally fixated upon her son. She may be dependent upon him for the affection which she has perhaps failed to receive from her husband. The anxiety she experiences in the dream may really be provoked by the thought that the emotional tie which binds her to her son is to be broken.

To sum up, this dream appears to embody a conflict in the dreamer's mind – between the fact that she regards her son as guilty of a 'crime' and her efforts to convince herself that the position is not so serious as she imagines it to be.

A complex analogous to the Oedipus complex in men is found in women, too. This is the Electra complex (although sometimes the term Oedipus complex is applied to both men and women). We have seen one half of the normal pair of dreams: the half embodying the punishment. Here is another half of a similar pair: the half embodying the crime. In this case the memory of the punishment dream was suppressed.

A 27-year-old married woman dreamed:

'My father, who died ten years ago, told me that he wanted me to have a baby by him. I told him that it was wrong and remember being terribly shocked.'

She produced the following thoughts in association with her dream:

'I very often dream of my father, whom I loved dearly. My husband and I have no children yet, but we hope to have some one day when we can afford to start a family.'

This dream is based upon the Electra complex. It takes its name from the Greek myth of Electra, whose father was murdered by her mother. Later Electra helped her brother Orestes to avenge her father's death by slaying her mother. Electra wanted to avenge her father's death because she was deeply attached to him, and this close attachment between father and daughter is the 'crime' embodied in the daughter's dream.

The attachment is so close that the dreamer would even like to have a child by her father. (The fact that he is dead is no obstacle to the dream mind, which is concerned only with wishes, not with realities.) We also note the shocked reaction of the dreamer's conscience to this idea. It justifies the conclusion that she must have had a dream in which the punishment for her 'crime' was depicted, even though she was unable to recall it.

We must also note two other wishes that are embedded in the dream. One is the wish that her father were still alive. Since she was greatly attached to him, it is easy to understand this wish. The dream attempts to gratify it by bringing her father to life again.

The second is the dreamer's wish to have a child by her husband. The father not only stands for himself but he also symbolizes the husband. The latter is the father-figure that a husband normally is to his wife. This wish, too, is easy to understand, seeing that the dreamer herself had admitted wanting to start a family when she could afford to do so.

The importance of emotions centring round the father-figure is further illustrated by another crime dream which will be described below. In this case the emotion was hostility, accompanied by the sense of guilt which hostility is apt to arouse.

A man dreamed that he was standing by the roadside watching a procession. An open car carrying the Prime Minister passed by, and as it drew level the dreamer took a Luger from his pocket and shot the Prime Minister dead. Turning round, the dreamer saw another man with a gun in his hand. This man fired at him and the dreamer fell to his bullet. As the dreamer lay unconscious on the ground, the other man admonished him for what he had done, but his voice was vague and indistinct and the dreamer could not make out a word he said.

The dream reminds us of the assassination of President Kennedy and of the events which followed that tragedy. It may indeed throw some light on the unconscious reasons why assassins strike down national leaders in real life. These leaders are father-figures to the people they lead, and as such they evoke the emotions of both affection and hatred which people have experienced in real life towards their own fathers.

This dream, then, symbolically gratifies the dreamer's repressed hostility against his father. It also symbolically atones for the feelings of guilt that this hostility arouses. Thus crime and punishment are combined in the one dream. The dreamer feels that nothing short of his own death will atone for what he has done, and the voice of his conscience (symbolized by the other gunman) reproves him as he pays the penalty for his crime. Even while paying the penalty, however, he attempts to suppress the reproaches of his conscience. This is seen in the fact that the voice is vague and indistinct. The dreamer claims that he cannot understand what it is saying. This implies that he does not wish to understand it. Always in dreams, what cannot be done is what the dreamer wishes not to do. The conflict between impulse and conscience is clearly reflected in this example of crime and punishment dreams.

The struggle between impulse and conscience provides fiction writers with some of their best material. This illustrates the fact that the fantasies embodied in novels, films, plays, etc., are all of a piece with those that sleep turns into dreams. They spring ultimately from the same unconscious source.

Let us consider an instance of this.

In 'The Andrew Hale Story', shown in the popular TV western series, *Wagon Train*, Major Seth Adams, the wagonmaster, played by the late Ward Bond, revealed that he had recurring dreams of being engaged in fighting redskins. Redskins or other strange or hostile elements symbolize the contents of the unconscious mind. The dreams suggest that Major Adams was engaged in a constant struggle with his repressed aggressive feelings, which emerged on those occasions when he got very angry, as he was often shown to do in the *Wagon Train* series.

These dreams are thus fully in keeping with his character, and the reference to them in 'The Andrew Hale Story' pointed to good psychological insight on the part of the writers of the series. His dreams also throw light on the unconscious reasons for Major Adams' choice of occupation. By leading the pioneers in their covered wagons on the western American frontier, he put himself in a position where he had a chance of objectifying his inner conflict. This he could do when the train was actually attacked by Red Indians and he could release his aggressive feelings in fighting them off.

We see, then, how intimately repressed impulses and the need of punishment which they provoke are linked in the imaginative products thrown up by the unconscious mind both in sleep and in waking life. These paired ideas expressed in both waking and sleeping fantasies are important for the understanding which they give us, not only of our own minds, but also of the psychology of the criminal.

CHAPTER NINE

THE FANTASY OF RESCUE

Mr R.M.G. said that on numerous occasions he had dreamed that he had been on Farewell Spit. This is a sand bar on the north-west tip of the south island of New Zealand, stretching approximately seventeen miles out to sea. 'In each dream', he added, 'I have been filled with a great sense of fear. I have visited Farewell Spit only once in my life, and as far as I'm objectively aware, I have no reason to fear it or even be interested enough to dream about it.'

Clearly, then, this sand bar must symbolize something else which Mr R.M.G. does fear. What can it be? Perhaps we should say rather that it symbolizes something which he wants, since dreams are really based on wishes, not fears. A dream arousing an intense feeling of fear embodies a wish that the dreamer has forbidden himself to entertain. The fear is the reaction of his conscience to the threatened emergence of the wish in the dream.

The question of what the sand bar meant to him is one which Mr R.M.G. was recommended to try to answer for himself. It was suggested that he should cast his mind back to the time when he visited it, and go on to trace the thoughts and memories of which the visit reminded him. He was assured that this process of free association was likely to recall something which would give a clue to the symbolic meaning of Farewell Spit.

Mr R.M.G. adopted this suggestion, as a result of which he was able to report: 'I feel I have the meaning of these dreams pretty well taped now. Casting my memory back to the visit I made to the Spit, I recall a small boat fishing some distance out from the shore. I remember the driver of our bus remarking that he wouldn't be out there in such a small boat for all the tea in China. The seas in this area are known to spring up very rapidly and with little warning.'

He also recalled that all the children at the small country school he attended were instructed in life-saving and artificial respiration. The former he could not grasp at all well and for this reason had been a source of much ridicule to the other children.

'On seeing this small boat', he continued, 'and hearing the driver's words, I recall wishing that the boat were closer inshore. I did not want this so that the occupant would be safe, but so that the boat would be nearer when it capsized. I could then go out and drag the semi-drowned occupant safely in. This would show the kids at school whether or not I could save lives!'

He thus interpreted his dreams as reflecting a desire to prove himself to his old schoolmates. He added: 'I think the fear in my dreams is the reaction of my conscience to the dreadful thought of risking a man's life just to gain, in fantasy, the confidence of my schoolmates.'

The dreamer, then, had unpleasant memories connected with life-saving drill at school. He used the wish that sprang from these incidents as the basis of the fantasy of rescue which he attempted to act out in his dreams. That is, he imagined himself going out and dragging to safety the occupant of the capsized boat. We don't actually see him doing this in his dreams. This is because conscience, which disapproves of the wish, censors its expression. All we are left with is the feeling of anxiety associated with the wish. This wish, which inspired his fantasy, served the purpose of compensating him for his feeling of inferiority, of enabling him to get his own back on the schoolmates who had ridiculed him.

One supposes, too, that the wish could be thought of in general terms as a longing to prove himself, not only to his schoolmates, but to the world at large.

This fantasy of rescue, upon which the dream of Mr R.M.G. was based, appears also in day-dreams. It is, in fact, one of several common types of day-dream, of which others are based on fantasies of display, grandeur, homage, conquest, and suffering.

'In phantasy', writes Freud, 'man can continue to enjoy a freedom from the grip of the external world, one which he has long relinquished in actuality ... The creation of the mental domain of phantasy has a complete counterpart in the establishment of "reservations" and "nature-parks" in places where the inroads of agriculture, traffic, or industry threaten to change the original face of the earth rapidly into something unrecognizable. The "reservation" is to maintain the old condition of things which has been regretfully sacrificed to necessity everywhere else; there everything may grow and spread as it pleases, including what is useless and even what is harmful. The mental realm of phantasy is also such a reservation reclaimed from the encroachments of the reality-principle.'

Here is an example of a day-dream which employs the fantasy of rescue. A man said he had a very vivid day-dream in which he saw the tractor worked by his brother-in-law overbalance and fall into a river. He saw himself dive in and swim out to his brother-in-law's aid. 'Underneath me all the time', he said, 'there were big sharks. I could never swim even half the distance in real life.'

This day-dream is based on the same saving fantasy as the dream of Mr R.M.G. By means of this fantasy the day-dreamer gives a boost to his ego. We see him attempting to perform some meritorious feat that would improve his opinion of himself and raise his esteem in the eyes of other people.

Another type of day-dream, closely allied to the fantasy of rescue, is the fantasy of display. For example, a young man said: 'I often imagine myself carrying out some great feat of heroism and having my name and a photo in the local paper commending me for bravery.' In this fantasy the day-dreamer, in circumstances at variance with real life, performs some feat which wins popular applause.

The general theme of other types of day-dream is much the same. That is, the day-dream compensates the day-dreamer for his frustration, for his feelings of inferiority, or for some other depressing circumstances which surround him in actuality.

For instance, in the fantasy of grandeur the day-dreamer becomes a conquering hero. 'I do a lot of day-dreaming', said a man of thirty-two, 'and sometimes I get so wrapped up in my day-dreams that I nearly meet with an accident. In these mental images I am always the conquering hero. But in real life I fall flat on my face in most of the things that I try to do.'

Another man stated: 'I often indulge in a fantasy of aggressive action. In particular, I find myself thinking up all kinds of situations in which I aggressively beat up whole gangs of ruffians or anyone else who dares to cross my path.'

A man of twenty-four reported a day-dream in which he became a conquering hero by saving his parents from death. As will be realized, this day-dream employs the fantasy of rescue as well as that of the conquering hero. At the same time as it cast him in the role of a hero, this fantasy also expressed the day-dreamer's hostility against his parents, whom he confessed to hating. By imagining himself saving them, however, he made retribution for the sense of guilt arising from the hostility which led him to imagine their coming close to death.

The following example clearly illustrates the role of the day-dream as a wish-fulfilling compensation for frustration experienced in the world of reality. Mr H.K.R., an 18-year-old clerk, said: 'I prefer to build for myself a world of fantasy in which I do the things and play the part that my self-consciousness denies to me in real life. When I can't avail myself of this sort of escapism, I become very depressed, anti-social, and sometimes suicidal.'

Another young man reported the following day-dreams: 'When I am walking to work or going out anywhere, I day-dream of situations in which people are crying for help while drowning or in a fire. It falls to me to rescue them. I also see myself as a great athlete winning every contest I go in for.'

The reality situation of this person presented a complete contrast. He admitted: 'In the past I have been a coward. I have an inferiority complex. Although I have courted two girls, I get doubts about whether I should marry. I have had these right from the very beginning of courtship. Every time I think of marriage I get a sudden fear that I cannot overcome. Somehow I don't feel manly enough to be able to face life. Several times since the age of fourteen I have felt an urge to do myself a terrible injury.'

These admissions throw an interesting light upon the way that the individual thinks of himself and upon the purpose which his day-dreams serve in the economy of his personality. The day-dreams suggest that his goal is to be admired. His attitude towards marriage shows that he shuns the more prosaic goal of co-operation with another in the joint adventure of marriage. Moreover, in his day-dreams he is compensating himself for his sense of inferiority. By imagining himself as an admired hero, he derives the sense of achievement that so far he has failed to obtain from his activities in real life. Yet deep within him there is a conviction that perhaps it might be better to end it all. This explains his obsession with doing himself an injury. If he did not succeed in doing away with himself, he might at least cripple himself in such a way as to evoke the pity and sympathy of other people. Thus, in either case his goal would be achieved.

Apart from its occurrence in dreams and day-dreams, one finds the fantasy of rescue cropping up in other quarters. It is interesting to speculate how much the poorer fiction would be without it. If novelists could not put their heroines into situations from which the hero could rescue them, they would indeed be at a loss to entertain their readers. This motif has proved a stand-by of the novel, the screen, and other forms of fictional entertainment ever since man began to divert his fellow man by spinning yarns out of the raw material of his fantasies.

The fantasy of rescue may also be observed in religion. One of the basic principles of the Christian religion is that God sent His Son into the world to save mankind from its sins. In the religions of the pagan world, too, gods and goddesses are conceived as playing the roles of rescuers or interveners in the affairs of humanity. We must assume that all this springs from man's own wishes to play the part of rescuer as well as to be rescued. Pleas addressed to the divinity in prayers and hymns are often couched in terms which imply the latter need especially.

These fantasies must be particularly prominent in the psychological make-up of persons who think of life in a particular way. Such persons are incapable of accepting a human relation as a partnership or collaboration of equals. To them one partner must be the rescuer, the other the rescued. For them life has become a kind of Orphean underworld in which they either go forth to save another from some impending disaster or else wait patiently to be saved themselves from such a contingency. They cast themselves either in the role of an Orpheus, who seeks by some magic spell to extricate another person from a dilemma, or in the role of a Eurydice, who awaits the satisfying prospect of being so extricated. These joint wishes on the part of the human race are embodied in the myths, poetry, religions, and dreams that have occupied and delighted man from early times with their charming naïveté and illusory sense of accomplishment.

CHAPTER TEN

DO DREAMS PREDICT THE FUTURE?

A fascinating bypath in psychology is the quest of a short cut to the interpretation of dreams. Some writers on this subject have conceived the possibility of classifying dream meanings as though they were definitions of words. This might be called the dictionary method of interpretation.

It is based upon the idea that dream symbols can be listed in alphabetical order, each accompanied by the meaning or meanings which are believed to attach to it. All the dreamer has to do is to pick out a prominent symbol from his dream, look it up in the dream dictionary, and there he can find what it means.

For example, a young woman dreamed: 'I was about to marry an old and repulsive man.' This dream is interpreted, dictionary fashion, under the heading of 'Marriage'. If you look up the entry for this theme in, say, Zolar's *Encyclopedia and Dictionary of Dreams*, you find that it lists a number of types of marriage dream. One of them is a woman dreaming of marriage to an old man. The meaning given for this dream is that sickness and trouble lie ahead.

This interpretation is open to three objections. One is that it assumes that dreams deal with the future. There may be some truth in this idea, but before we assume that there is, we should attempt to relate them to the past. The second objection is that no evidence is advanced to support the statement that sickness and trouble are the particular events that the future holds. Thirdly, according to the dreamer herself, the interpretation is untrue.

The dreamer's interpretation of her own dream was revealed in her associations, which were: 'Ever since I was fourteen, I have been afraid that I might not marry. I felt that I should be left on the shelf, or that I should have to marry someone old and not very nice just for the sake of security. Perhaps my need of security is not satisfied and in my mind I connect old men with money and the security which that implies.'

These associations show that the dreamer's thoughts and the meaning of her dream are not concerned with sickness and trouble but with security. The old and repulsive man does not symbolize a threatening figure but something towards which the dreamer is attracted in the present. The dream reflects her wish for security, which she identifies with marriage to an old man.

Orthodox dream interpretation rejects the view that the meaning of a dream can be arrived at by consulting a dream dictionary without reference to the dreamer's personal background. Dr Sándor Ferenczi has summed up this criticism as follows: 'It would be an enticing problem to collect the fragments of dreams that can be explained symbolically and to write a modern dream-book, in which the explanation could be found for the separate parts of dreams. This is not possible, however.'

Should we also reject the view that dreams predict the future? Before we can answer this question, we must establish the facts. There is little point in discussing it unless we are sure that apparent predictive dreams do occur.

'Freud has probably solved many of the riddles of dream-life', says Dr Oskar Pfister (*Some Applications of Psycho-Analysis*), '– no doubt the most important of them. But several important problems of dream psychology still remain unsolved.' Although he does not mention it, this is one of them.

In Freud's paper on 'The Occult Significance of

Dreams' we read: 'There can, indeed, be no doubt that there are such things as prophetic dreams, in the sense that their content gives some sort of picture of the future; the only question is whether these predictions coincide to any noticeable extent with what really happens subsequently.'

We shall attempt to establish the facts by means of examples of a particular kind: those in which the result of a horse-race is seen in a dream that occurs before the event.

Horse-race dreams have been chosen because, by simplifying the problem, they enable us to come to grips with it better. Such a dream can be compared more readily with the subsequent event than can other types of predictive dreams. We need ask ourselves only one question: Did the horse win the race or not? By answering this question in a clear-cut manner, a dream of this type fulfils the condition of simplification that is desirable in examining this problem.

Naturally, it is not the only type of predictive dream, but other types may confuse the issue. They may contain several elements, some of which resemble the subsequent event and some of which do not. Thus we are left in doubt as to whether the dream was really predictive. In the case of a horse-race dream there is no doubt.

For example, a lady from Birmingham reported dreams about a certain horse winning a big race, which, in fact, it did win. 'At the time', she declared, 'I was not at all interested in horse-racing and knew nothing about it.'

A Sunday newspaper announced that a 35-year-old Halifax woman dreamed twelve hours before the race that Pinza would win the Derby, as indeed the horse did.

On the morning of another Derby Day a man dreamed that he heard the names of the first two winners announced. He was so impressed that, although not normally interested in racing, he watched the race on TV and was surprised to find that his dream was correct.

'Some years ago on the night before a big race', said a 49-year-old bricklayer, 'I saw in my dream the horses passing the winning-post and heard their names called out. I wrote down the names of the first three horses at the breakfast table. My premonition was correct. I do not take any interest in horse-racing and I never bet on horses.'

'I seldom ever bet on horses', stated another man, 'but on the eve of the Lincoln I fell asleep thinking of the race. I had a dream and it was very distinct. I remember standing at a bar at the racecourse. Over the P.A. system I heard a voice distinctly announcing as the winner number six, second number five. I repeated the numbers several times. Then I awoke. I recounted the dream at the breakfast table. That afternoon the saddle-cloth on the winner of the Lincoln was number six and on the second horse number five.'

According to the press, a 26-year-old housewife dreamed in four years the winners of several classic races, although before she went to bed she did not know the names of any of the horses entered for them. Before she began to have these dreams, she had had no interest in racehorses and had never placed a bet.

She dreamed that she was holidaying at Cloncarrig, although she had never been to Ireland. A horse of this name won the Grand National. In the case of Sheila's Cottage, another Grand National winner, she dreamed of the jockey's colours, black and white. She dreamed that she was calling to her baby, 'Come here, my love'. The next day My Love won the Derby.

The case in favour of the view that predictive dreams do occur receives strong support from the examples cited above. A body of evidence, of which these cases are typical, is gradually accumulating to suggest that, in a minority of dreams at least, 'coming events cast their shadows before'. The weight of this evidence cannot lightly be set on one side.

Nevertheless, we shall now proceed to demolish the case that we have thus carefully built up in support of the view that the future can be predicted in dreams. We shall do this by showing that for every so-called predictive dream there is a dream which appeared to be predictive but was not.

We have cited eight dreams in which the future appeared to be predicted; we shall now cite eight more in which the future definitely failed to be predicted.

A national daily newspaper announced that its tipster (The Scout) 'saw' the 'winner' of the Manchester November Handicap in a dream a fortnight before the race was run. The horse in question was the favourite, Western Window, which in the dream won the race by half a length. Western Window was placed eighth in the actual race.

A colleague of the present writer told him that he had dreamed of reading in the stop-press column of a newspaper that Royal Tan had won the Grand National at 26-1. Some weeks later it became known that the horse did not even run, being withdrawn before the race.

A young man dreamed of a race in which two horses were competing for the lead. The horse which finally won the race in the young man's dream was called Twenty Twenty. When on the following morning he consulted the list of runners at a race-meeting to be held that day, he found that a horse of this name was entered. The horse did not win.

A woman dreamed that a certain horse would win the Grand National. Her prediction turned out to be correct. The following year she again dreamed the 'winner' of this race. The horse was an also-ran. The next year, too, she had a dream in which she saw the Grand National 'winner'. Again the horse was an also-ran.

Another man dreamed that a race was won by a horse called Baire. His hopes were dashed when Baire was unplaced in the actual race.

The last two examples are taken from an article entitled 'The Man Who Dreamt Winners', which appeared in *Reader's Digest*.

After recounting a number of dreams in which he forecast winners, the author, John Godley, goes on to say: 'I dreamt that I was walking down the street when I heard a radio in a shop transmitting an account of the running of the Cambridgeshire. I hastened to listen, but the broadcast ended. I asked a man, "Do you know what horse won?"

' "Claro won", he replied in a very offhand way, and the dream ended.

'Next day I bet on Claro and then listened with friends to the broadcast of the race. Claro was unplaced. He never for a moment seemed a likely winner.'

Subsequently Godley dreamed both a winner and a loser. In his dream he saw in the following day's paper that Monk's Mistake and Pretence had won. Towards the finish of the actual race the first horse was neck and neck with another, but, losing ground owing to a mistake at the last jump, failed to win. The other horse that appeared in the dream won his race.

What conclusions, if any, can we draw from this discussion? It seems reasonable to suppose that the idea of predictive dreams gains currency in a simple way. We are entitled to infer that those dreams which appear to predict the future have greater news value than those which fail to predict it.

We hear more about the former – both at the time of the dream and after the event has confirmed it. The other sort, however, are soon forgotten when the event fails to confirm them. In other words, the idea that dreams predict the future gains currency through stressing the cases that support it and ignoring those which do not.

When we look into the matter more closely, however, we find that dreams which do not predict the future are just as numerous as those which do. Hence it may be that we cannot attach any particular significance to the latter except as mere coincidences. If dreams do indeed predict the future, we may have to look for other grounds on which to support the contention.

The position is summed up as follows by Freud in the paper which we have already mentioned: 'The notion that there is any mental power, apart from acute calculation, which can foresee future events in detail is on the one hand too much in contradiction to all the expectations and presumptions of science and on the other hand corresponds too closely to certain ancient and familiar human desires which criticism must reject as unjustifiable pretensions.'

Which of us would not like to win a fortune by being given the results of horse-races in his dreams? But at present, however, this prospect still lies in the realms of fond hopes and easy delusions.

In spite of this the problem is worth looking into further and this we shall proceed to do in the next chapter.

CHAPTER ELEVEN

WARNING DREAMS

'Recently', said Miss C.I., 'a friend of mine dreamed that she saw me killed in a car accident. She told me of this dream because she said it might be a warning for me to be extra careful when driving. I must admit this is worrying me. It would have been better if I had been left in ignorance.'

'Do you believe it is possible', she went on, 'for some people to have warnings in dreams? About a week before this particular dream, I was in conversation with my friend, and we talked about driving and the dangers of the road.'

One feels that it is rather difficult to answer Miss C.I.'s question with a plain 'yes' or 'no'. If one answers 'yes', it is hardly likely to relieve her worry. On the other hand, if one answers 'no', this ignores the fact that warning dreams have been known to occur.

There are, however, two other possible explanations. One is that her friend's positive feelings for her are mixed with an element of hostility, which is gratified in her dream by imagining that Miss C.I. has had an accident. An objection to this view may be that the friendship contains no such element. This could be true, of course. The second possible explanation takes this objection into account. It is that in her friend's dream, Miss C.I. symbolizes someone else against whom the dreamer does feel hostile. The dreamer replaces that person with Miss C.I. because there may be some superficial resemblance between the two of them. The replacement would also be a means by which the dreamer conceals from herself the identity of the person against whom she feels hostile.

The point of this discussion is that the scientific method requires us first to look into possible natural explanations before we consider supernatural ones which imply that the future can be foretold. Nevertheless, even when we do this, we appear to leave an unexplained residue of premonitory dreams which strongly suggest a paranormal knowledge of events to come.

Such ideas have always intrigued and fascinated the inquiring mind, and for ages men have pondered this enigma of reaching into the unknown future. Writing over a hundred years ago, Joseph Haven said in his *Mental Philosophy*: 'Some law, not fully known to us, may exist, by virtue of which the nervous system, when in a highly excited state, becomes susceptible of impressions not ordinarily received and is put in communication, in some way to us mysterious, with scenes, places, and events, far distant, so as to become strangely cognizant of the coming future. Can any one show that this is impossible?'

Indeed, no one could show that it was impossible in Haven's day, and now a hundred years later the position remains unchanged. We are still no nearer solving the problem which such dreams present. A conservative view of the position might even claim it has yet to be established that there is a problem to solve. Our inability to explain all dreams in naturalistic terms may simply be a measure of our ignorance rather than an indication that there are dreams which lie outside the naturalistic frame of reference.

The chief difficulty that has no doubt deterred psychologists from the study and investigation of predictive dreams is that the problem bristles with puzzling philosophical implications. If the future can be predicted in dreams, then in some incomprehensible way it must already exist. But if the future already exists, what becomes of free will? The concept of free will may well have to be abandoned as an illusion arising from our imperfect comprehension of the nature of time.

This is a view towards which psychological determinism leans. This doctrine holds that all actions are determined by definite causes. The feeling of free will arises from the capacity of the conscious mind to observe its own operation. Of the many conflicting impulses that strive for supremacy in our minds, the one that succeeds in winning it is conceived as our free will. What we perceive, however, is only a small part of what actually occurs in our mind. 'Of course', remarked the late Dr A.A. Brill, 'there is no such thing [as free will] in psychiatry or in the natural sciences. Everything must be determined.'

Let us cite one or two further examples of the type of dream we are discussing.

Mr R.J. suffered a severed head injury as a result of a motor-cycle accident in which he collided with a bridge. 'Before I had the accident', he declared, 'I sometimes dreamed of going into this bridge, which I used to pass over on the journey to and from work.'

In his book *An Experiment with Time* J.W. Dunne tells of a dream that he had in the autumn of 1913. In his dream he saw a high railway embankment which he recognized as being a little way north of the Firth of Forth Bridge. Below on the grass, groups of people were walking about. A train had fallen over the embankment.

He formed the impression that the accident was to occur the following spring. He and his sister, to whom he told the dream, jokingly decided to warn their friends against travelling north at that time.

The sequel came on 14 April 1914 when the Flying Scotsman was derailed north of the Forth Bridge and crashed down an embankment on to the golf links below.

One night at his RAF camp, a young man dreamed

that his aunt came and stood by his bed. He woke up and noted that the time was 2.30 a.m. Some days later he learned that his aunt had died on the same day and at the same hour as his dream.

Let us examine the last of the above examples in closer detail. Could it be that at the time when the aunt was dying she was thinking of her nephew, and the thought communicated itself to his mind, in which it created her image? This explanation, if indeed it can be regarded as such, would mean that the dream was based on telepathy.

On the other hand, clairvoyance might be the explanation. This would mean that the nephew received in his sleep an impression of his aunt – an impression which was not based upon information derived through any of the ordinary senses. This impression could have worked itself into his dream.

The ordinary type of dream is, as we have seen in previous chapters, a wish-fulfilment. The possibility of treating the above example as such should not be excluded. For example, the young man may have known that his aunt was ill and that it was feared she might die. In this case, the dream could perhaps be interpreted as embodying a wish on his part that she should live, a wish which the dream gratified by showing her alive.

The weakness of this interpretation is that it does not explain why the dream should occur at the same time and on the same day as the aunt died. It compels us to dismiss this circumstance as a coincidence – which is rather less than it seems to be.

Nevertheless, if we can apply the wish-fulfilment theory to an apparently premonitory dream, the scientific principle of economy demands that we should do so. Here is another example in which this proved to be possible. In his biography of the occultist Aleister Crowley, *The Great Beast* (Rider, 1955), John Symonds quotes from Crowley's diary where he says that two nights before his mother's death he dreamed that she had died. At first sight the dream might be taken to be predictive, but Crowley goes on to say that he often dreamed that his mother had died. Since he admitted that he hated his mother, the dream must clearly be understood as gratifying his hostility against her rather than as predicting her death.

As we see from this example, apparent warning dreams may occur without their being fulfilled immediately. A mother once told me that a few weeks previously she had dreamed that her daughter would be killed on such-and-such a date. The date came and went and the daughter was still alive. In this case we are obliged to look for an explanation other than premonition. We can find it in the wish-fulfilment theory. This mother had had the unfortunate experience of losing her first child. 'Our first baby', she said, 'died when he was a few days old.' Having had this experience, she unconsciously feared that she would lose the second child also. To relieve the tension and anxiety created by this fear, she imagined her daughter dying in her dream. It is as though she were saying to herself: 'I can't stand the anxiety of waiting for it to happen, so I will bring it about myself.' This is what she did in fantasy by imagining that her daughter would be killed.

The wish-fulfilment theory implies that dreams deal with the past and not with the future. Yet it is not unusual to find persons inclined to dispute this point of view. For instance, Mr R.A.E. pointed out that he had several times noticed his dreams warning him of the future. He cited a dream that he had a month before he left school. This warned him to be prepared to go to another country, and on leaving school this is what actually happened to him. 'This and many other dreams', he concluded, 'do not make clear to me your statement that dreams deal with the past and not the future.'

Yet this view can be defended in spite of the dreams that appear to contradict it. We must assume that at the time of the dream the above dreamer's thoughts would naturally be concerned with what was going to happen to him after he left school. Possibly he may even have harboured a wish to go to another country. In this case the dream cannot be considered as a premonition, except in the sense that both the dream and the future event were the outcome of the dreamer's wish.

'You may know', writes Daniel A. Simmons, 'of some dream that "came true". An idea produced by a dream may realize itself under proper conditions, just as any other idea may so realize itself; and the mystery and superstition clustering about dreams tend to produce just the proper conditions for this realization.'

Nevertheless, there do seem to be a few dreams predicting future events that are independent of human wishes. The explanation of such dreams is by no means clear. They seem to require us to assume that the dream mind is stored with knowledge of the future as well as of the past. For the moment, however, such a view must be suspect. The premonitory dream really warns us to temper speculation with caution.

CHAPTER TWELVE

DREAMS IN COLOUR

'A few years ago', said Mr T.H., 'I used to dream in Technicolor. I recall being of a very happy nature at the time.'

According to Professor Calvin Hall, who has collected records of many thousands of dreams, about two-thirds of all dreams are in black and white. 'Only one dream in three', he writes, 'is coloured, or has some colour in it.'

A few people, he adds, dream entirely in colour; a few never experience colour in their dreams; the majority sometimes dream in colour, but oftener do not.

This view is not shared by Gladys Mayer, who in *Colour and Healing* (New Knowledge Books) maintains that all dreams are coloured. Just as we all dream but don't all remember our dreams, so, thinks this writer, we all dream in colour but don't all remember the colours.

'Another much more brilliant colour world opens for us when we fall asleep', continues Gladys Mayer, 'and again not all people are conscious of it. One often hears or reads discussions about whether dreams are coloured. Some people, even some painters, assert that dreams are in monochrome, like a photograph ...'

Miss Mayer remembers dreaming as a child of three great tawny lions in a reddish desert against a brilliant blue sky. 'Nothing could shake my certainty thereafter', she writes, 'that dreams are coloured, until in later life this awareness of colour in dreams awoke again. Yet our faculty for perceiving colours the moment our eyes are closed dies, if it is not cherished.'

In *Heaven and Hell* (Chatto & Windus) Aldous Huxley thinks that to be effective, dream symbols do not require to be coloured. Symbols embody psychological conflicts which can be expressed just as readily without colour. In support of this view he adds: 'It is worth remarking that, in most people's experience, the most brightly coloured dreams are those of landscapes, in which there is no drama, no symbolic reference to conflict, merely the presentation to consciousness of a given, non-human fact.'

There is no satisfactory psychological explanation of the presence of colour in dreams. 'We have come to the conclusion', writes Dr Hall, 'that colour in dreams yields no information about the personality of the dreamer.' However, various theories have been put forward.

One emerges from what Huxley is quoted as saying above. He believes, as we have said, that where symbols express psychological conflicts, colour is not needed. Therefore, in his view, the dreams in which colour occurs are those that embody no conflict. A major objection to this theory is that all dreams appear to embody a conflict of some kind.

Secondly, there is the theory which relates colour in dreams to some diseased physical condition of the dreamer. This theory was put forward by Édouard Saby, who in *L'avenir révélé à tous* (Éditions Jean Vitiano) says that dreams in which one finds an excess of green indicate a disorder of the liver. Those in which one finds an excess of red warn us against the possibility of haemorrhage.

'According to Meunier and Masselon,' he writes, 'cardiac and circulatory troubles determine dreams in which this colour predominates (blood, flames). Artigues cites the case of a woman who for a long time dreamed of blood and flames in such distressing nightmares that she had herself examined by a doctor. She was found to have been suffering from endocarditis.'

A third theory is that colour in dreams is related to the

dreamer's artistic talent.

For example, a lady who experienced dreams in colours said: 'I have always been colour-conscious. My father was an art master. I always see very clearly the tone in a colour. The blue or gold that is in red and green is just as vivid as the primary colour. In childhood my artistic talents were discouraged and repressed to the point of extinction by my mother, who suffered considerably from one impecunious artist in the family and did not wish to have another.'

In this case we might assume that the lady's dreams in colour gave an outlet to the artistic talent repressed in her childhood.

Gladys Mayer says that her students often tell her that their painting lessons start them dreaming in colour. This suggests that dreams in colour, besides releasing repressed artistic talents, also provide an outlet for those of which the dreamer is fully aware.

From this Miss Mayer draws the natural conclusion. 'One might then expect', she adds, 'that all painters would dream in colour. That very many do is evident through modern surrealist painters cultivating dream consciousness as their inspiration. But the quality of their sleep or dream experience is influenced by the subjects they give attention to in waking life, be it form, colour, pattern, or dark and light.'

The present writer's view of dreams in colour is that they hark back to childhood and evoke some childish emotion. To the child, colours appear so much brighter and fresher than to the adult. In other words, the dreamer is reviving memories and feelings which he first had as a child. As Wordsworth puts it in his *Ode on Intimations of Immortality*:

> There was a time when meadow, grove, and stream,
> The earth, and every common sight,
> To me did seem

Apparell'd in celestial light,
The glory and the freshness of a dream.

The colours that appear in a dream set its emotional tone. For example a 48-year-old housewife dreamed:

'I am in a square courtyard with very high and dark walls and a narrow alley leading to the open air – with something very brightly coloured falling from the sky. Sometimes I am alone, sometimes with a crowd of strangers. Different things fall – stars, balloons, rockets, etc. I am always petrified with fear.'

'I had to give up a very full life', she said, 'and take a post where I could live at home. When I married, I was quite content to give up every other interest. I did only what I was told. I made few friends. I thought I was quite happy. My husband told me what I must and must not say to people. I have spent only one night away from home. I was asked if I would go back to teaching, but my husband refused to let me. I have no self-confidence at all.'

A mass of brightly coloured objects falling from the sky suggests an ambivalent mood which the dreamer's associations confirm, i.e., she is petrified with fear in the dream but happy about the situation which it depicts.

This dream represents fairly faithfully the dreamer's current situation. The high walls which surround her symbolize the restrictions under which she lives. A hopeful sign is the fact that there is a way out from the courtyard, leading to the free air of liberty. The dream shows, however, that she is not yet ready to leave her prison. As she herself puts it, 'I have no self-confidence at all.'

A crowd of strangers, Freud tells us, signifies a secret. This illustrates the law of association by contrast, for a secret is known to one or two persons only. The secret is, of course, hidden from the dreamer's conscious mind, although her unconscious mind (dream mind) knows it, i.e., the reason why she has 'put herself in jail'.

A piece of additional evidence in support of the view that dreams in colour deal with childhood matters is to be seen in the dreams of a 73-year-old widow, who said: 'For some time I dreamed of going into strange houses and not being able to find my way out again. The first of these was gaily coloured and peopled with Chinese actors with their faces vividly painted like masks.' Her associations were: 'I remember that when I was a child my *amah* took me behind the stage of a Chinese theatre. She no doubt thought·it would amuse me, but it terrified me. My parents never knew about this tour of inspection.'

Her comments on this dream confirm the impression that such dreams refer to childhood, when the world seems dressed in so much brighter colours. Her dream revives a particular experience of childhood, namely, that of going behind the stage of the Chinese theatre. If dreams are wish-fulfilments, why should she dream about something that terrified her? The answer is that she still wishes it had not frightened her, because if she had not been afraid it would have made it easier to tell her parents. The dream suggests that she was reviving the experience to give herself a second chance of coming to terms with the emotions which it inspired.

At the present time we cannot decide among these various theories, for each has its advantages and disadvantages. For example, probably many people who are ill do not have dreams in colour, so their physical condition cannot be reflected in them. Again, probably some people who have dreams in colour do not have any artistic talent. A criticism of the present writer's theory is that dreams in colour are not the only ones that relate to childhood emotions. This is also true of some dreams in black and white.

Therefore, we must leave the subject in very much the position in which we picked it up. We cannot say that one theory is right and the others wrong. Further research into the problem will no doubt succeed in throwing further light upon its origins. In the meantime we can only sit back – or rather lie back – and enjoy coloured dreams for their intrinsic beauty and the pleasurable emotions they excite.

CHAPTER THIRTEEN

WAKING DREAMS

A few years ago, having to stay overnight in London, I put up at an hotel near Marble Arch. The room I booked had an adjoining bathroom. A door, which I thought was closed when I went to bed, separated the two.

In the early hours I awoke and sat up in bed with a sense of alarm. Staring round the bathroom door was the face of a sinister-looking man. I rubbed my eyes, hardly believing what I saw. I looked again and the face was still there, but by the time I put the light on it had gone.

I got out of bed and went into the bathroom. I was the sole occupant of both rooms. The bathroom door was open, but the bathroom window was closed and showed no signs of having been opened. I went back to bed, distinctly puzzled.

My wife had had a similar experience at an hotel in Llandudno some years before. We were on holiday at the time with our two children, both of whom shared our room. The younger girl was sleeping in a cot. One night my wife woke up to see the figure of a woman bending over the cot. This figure, too, vanished after a shorter interval than my own waking dream, which had lasted about ten seconds.

I didn't actually share this experience with my wife, as I remained asleep while it was going on, but she told me about it in the morning.

What we saw must have been the final images of dreams which persisted for a few seconds after we awoke. The main parts of the dreams, of which these few residues survived, were forgotten, as we know that many dreams are.

The classic case of a 'waking dream', which has aroused more controversy than any other, is the report contained in *An Adventure* by the Oxford lady dons Miss Moberly and Miss Jourdain, who visited Versailles in 1901.

There they had a remarkable experience in which they saw what was believed to be a re-enactment of events occurring in the time of Marie Antoinette. They asked the way from men wearing three-cornered hats, a man in a dark cloak with a pock-marked face, and a woman sketching in a white hat.

This 'adventure' has long been held to be a true psychic experience in spite of attempts to give it a purely natural explanation. One such attempt was based on Philippe Jullian's book *Robert de Montesquiou.* Montesquiou was a French count who had moved into a house near the Petit Trianon just before the two English ladies' visit to Versailles. He was in the habit of dressing up, had been given the key to the park, and was probably entertaining friends dressed in eighteenth-century costumes. This 'explanation' has been challenged on the grounds that it is not hard evidence and that to be seen near Paris in August, the month of the Misses Moberly and Jourdain's visit, would have been 'social death' for Montesquiou and his friends.

Although it does not apply to the above experience, we have suggested that a vision or hallucination can occur because a dream image persists briefly after awaking. But similar visions can also occur as we lie in bed before going to sleep. We mentioned this point briefly in Chapter Two, where we referred to such hallucinations as 'hypnagogic'.

Several features combine to make these visions remarkable. One is that the images are often brightly coloured. For instance, a married 41-year-old building manager reported: 'While I lie in bed before going to

sleep, I see gaudily coloured foliage dancing in front of
my eyes. If this had happened only once, I should have
dismissed it, but it happens regularly. The pictures are
quite vivid and the scenes always seem to be tropical. I am
awake at the time. Try as I may, I cannot drive them
away. Strangely enough, I am normally incapable of
seeing a mental picture'.

Miss J.M.H. said: 'Quite frequently, and particularly
when resting in the afternoons, I experience dreams.
They do not appear to be dreams in the true sense of the
word in that I am conscious of all that is going on around
me. Yesterday afternoon, for instance, I "dreamed" that
I was bidding for a large house at an auction. When I
walked out of the house, I saw a truly superb seascape,
which even now I can visualize in detail. It was certainly
not reminiscent of anything I have seen in a picture nor
along any of our coasts. Whilst I was looking at this
scene, a man came up and stood beside me. He repeated
a quotation: "Only that which is retained in the heart
can ..." – the rest I have forgotten.

'The foregoing is the most recent but only one of many
such "dreams" I have had in this twilight state.'

Besides vivid natural scenes, faces appear in
hypnagogic visions. 'Very frequently', said Mr C.J.O'N.,
'when I lie down at night, I am afflicted by visions of a
series of ever-changing faces – all sorts of weird faces
merging one into another. Sometimes they leer and grin
horribly, and sometimes they are strong, clearly defined,
bearded, biblical faces.

'This can continue for upwards of an hour. During all
this time I am wide awake. The sensation is unpleasant,
to say the least of it. Is there a psychological reason for
those visitations?'

Hypnagogic visions are usually in visual terms. That
is, their content is seen. In the following report Mrs
I.M.W. describes hypnagogic visions containing images

derived from hearing and smell as well as sight:

'When in bed I see in the wall a round window through which I not only see but hear all sorts of things. One morning I saw hundreds of bluebottles and could hear them buzzing Another morning I saw a farmyard with a shippen and two large green doors. At the left was a brown and white cow, on the right a black and white one. The brown one was mooing and it jumped over the door. As it jumped, the door opened and inside were stalls with four more cows. Another night I saw the river bank full of roses. I could even smell them. I've seen fields full of horses. I've seen and heard aircraft. I say to my husband, "I wonder what I'll see in my window to-night!"'

Can it be that persons who report hypnagogic visions are reliving experiences that they have gone through in the past? These might be experiences of so long ago that they have forgotten them. But in the waking state that precedes sleep some unusual condition of the mind may allow the buried memories to come to the surface again.

For example, the faces seen by Mr C.J.O'N. might be memory images of the faces of persons who bent over and grinned at him as he lay in his pram in infancy. Biblical imagery, too, impresses itself on the child's mind with significant vividness in childhood. Here is another report which may be basically derived from the same source.

Mrs E.A.C. reported: 'Some time ago I awoke early one morning. I was amazed that very suddenly a picture appeared. In it I saw Christ toiling up a hill, wearing a loose white garment, a crown of thorns on his head and the cross upon his back. He was accompanied by a powerfully-built, dark-skinned man, and behind was a long line of people.'

She added that she had never seen a painting or print resembling the vision. It might be, however, that, although she had seen such a painting, she could not at the moment recall it. Alternatively, she may have created a mental picture of something which she had read, probably from the Bible. It agrees with the account given by John, who says that Christ carried his own cross, whereas the other Gospel writers say that it was carried for him by Simon of Cyrene. Luke records a detail which appears in the vision, i.e., 'Great numbers of people followed' (Luke 23,27).

The fact that no external object exists is not important if you have ever experienced an hallucination. For you the hallucinated image is just as real as perceiving something in reality.

Your belief in the reality of what you have seen is encouraged by the intensity or vividness of the experience. But, above all, it is determined by something within you just as the dreams of sleep are. It does not mean that your judgment is unbalanced or that your intelligence is being called in question.

Nevertheless, when the mind plays tricks of this kind on you, you ask yourself: What can I do about it? Where images are constantly enriching your experience and promoting artistic, musical, or literary inspiration, it would, of course, be a pity to try to stop them. You would impoverish your inner life by doing so.

But where they are causing you alarm or even panic – and some can be quite alarming – you can help yourself by bearing this point in mind:

When confronted with some mental phenomenon which you don't understand, look for a simple explanation. Bear in mind that many such experiences are memories. At some time we have had these experiences in reality but have forgotten them until the memories of them are, in some unusual mental state, revived in the form of the hypnagogic vision or waking dream.

CHAPTER FOURTEEN

INSIGHT AND SELF-KNOWLEDGE

The strengthening of insight and self-knowledge is one of the most important creative functions of the dream. Sometimes the dream reveals the dreamer to himself or herself in a general way; at other times the help received may take the form of self-acquired understanding of some particular problem, such as the origin of a nervous breakdown. Both types of case are illustrated in the instances that follow.

A young man said that he felt unsure of himself and lacked confidence in his ability to make a success of his job.

He reported the following dream: 'The setting is the site of a large, partly-constructed building where I am employed by a building firm. I remember walking about clad in a thick duffle coat and protective helmet. Presently I begin to feel extremely tired and sleepy; so I walk over to a hut, observe that no one is looking, lie down, make myself comfortable, and fall asleep. I am awakened by one of my superiors who, quite naturally, inquires why I am sleeping when I should be busy at my work. I hurriedly hunt for an excuse which soon comes. I tell him that I have a cold and am not feeling at all well. This is not true but he accepts it, telling me to take a few days off to aid my recovery.'

The dreamer's own analysis of his dream was as follows: 'The fact that I fall asleep and am found out indicates that I am afraid that I do not pay enough attention to my responsibilities.'

The theme of this dream is that of 'lying down on the job'. The dream mind often shows a literal

representation of such figurative ideas. The dreamer is
accusing himself of wanting to neglect his duties. The
accusation is put into the mouth of his superior, who
inquires about the reason for his conduct. This superior
symbolizes his own conscience. (Conscience is a superior
moral agency which passes judgment, just as a superior
at work is entitled to do.)

The dream expresses that side of the dreamer's self
which says that, because he feels uncertain about his
ability to do the job, he would rather not do it at all. The
repressed wish to escape from the job without having to
blame himself is fulfilled by putting the advice to give up
the work into the mouth of his superior.

A married 44-year-old chartered accountant had a
nervous breakdown. The doctor who treated him said
that his trouble was that he did not have the strength of
will to disappoint others, and so he tried to do too much
all the time. A psychiatrist had told him that he was far
too concerned about the opinions of his clients and tried
too hard to please everybody.

He reported a dream as follows: 'A lay preacher is
about to begin his sermon. He announces that there is a
girl in church who has a special problem and that he
proposes to deal with this problem publicly in his
sermon. No sooner has he begun than another girl gets
up and takes the first girl out. Immediately the
congregation begin to reproach the preacher, who,
realizing how much pain he has caused, breaks down
and cries, protesting that he meant no harm. I find
myself sitting among the accusers and my condemnation
is stronger than anyone else's.'

He recalled the following associations: 'I used to be a
lay preacher before I had the nervous breakdown, when I
had to give up all outside engagements. When I was
young, my father was very strict and pressed us to get on
in the world by study. He used to make us uncomfortable

at times by exposing our follies publicly to goad us on, all in good part, I suppose. I now realize that he was on the wrong track, although meaning well.'

This invites us to assume that the lay preacher in his dream is himself, or perhaps we should say it is one part of himself, since another part is also present ('I find myself sitting among the accusers').

The dream suggests that the excessive concern about the opinions of other people, which the psychiatrist found in him, is a defence against a repressed wish to cause them pain, which is gratified by airing a private matter in public.

This cannot be done without provoking feelings of guilt, which demand a self-imposed punishment to atone for them.

This self-inflicted punishment is imagined in the dream in the form of the condemnation which the lay preacher incurs from his congregation, the congregation representing the 'other people' on whose good opinion he is excessively dependent. The breakdown in the pulpit symbolizes his nervous breakdown, produced, the dream says, by feelings of guilt about the repressed wish to cause pain.

The dreamer plays a double role in the dream as both accused and accuser. The accused is that part of himself which unconsciously wishes to cause pain (the lay preacher); the accuser is his conscience (symbolized by the self whose condemnation is stronger than anyone else's).

We may conclude that the wish to cause pain, reflected in the dream, is an act of revenge for the pain which his father caused him. In the dream he imagines himself 'getting his own back' by exposing someone else publicly, just as he himself had been exposed publicly as a child. For a time he takes on the role of the father, castigating another as he himself had been castigated.

A middle-aged married woman said: 'I have been making an effort to understand my fears and uncertainties, and I was wondering whether my dreams give a clue to some of them. I have remembered three and have written them down. Do they mean anything to you?'

The dreams were as follows:

1. 'I went to see my sister, who has a baby girl ten days old. The baby came walking to meet me, behaving and dressed like a four-year-old.'

2. 'I was in a car park en route for somewhere with my husband. He told me that he would have to take over the night-watch in the office. Furious that he would lose his sleep with a long journey ahead of us, I went to the office to complain, but no one would listen. Then, when we tried to park the car, we had to push it up a steep gravel slope. We pushed and pushed, but always the gravel slipped back.'

3. 'We went for a picnic near water. A spoon fell in and was floating. My daughter tried to get it and fell in. The water became a torrent sweeping into a cavern. I jumped in to save her. Then she was above me and jumped in to save me. We were both safe, but could still see the water going underground.'

In the first dream the baby is coming to meet the dreamer. Presumably she has substituted her sister's daughter for her own daughter. The dream hints at the possibility that she wishes that her daughter were more dependent upon her (as a child is upon an adult when learning to walk), or that she were willing to meet her mother half way.

This idea seems to be repeated in the third dream, in which she imagines her daughter depending upon her to save her from the consequences of her own action. The mother pictures her daughter as falling. In dreams, as we have seen in Chapter Five, the literal act of falling often has a moral or emotional significance: it symbolizes falling into temptation, falling in love, etc. When the dreamer attempts to rescue her daughter, she finds that their roles are reversed: the daughter becomes in a position to save her. So it looks as though, besides wishing her daughter to be dependent upon her, the mother is to some extent dependent upon her daughter.

Two dreams may be complementary in the sense that what is disguised in one may be shown openly in the other. This point, which was discussed in Chapter Six, is illustrated by the first and third dreams. Thus, in the first dream the woman's daughter is disguised as her sister's daughter, and the dreamer's wish that her daughter should need her is disguised as the action of the child coming to meet her. In the third dream, on the other hand, both the daughter and the dependence of one person upon another are shown openly.

What are we to make of the second dream? Here there seems to be a wish to get out of some difficult situation involving the dreamer and her husband. The conflict in this dream is between the wish to continue their journey (in dreams a journey symbolizes the dreamer's journey through life) and her inability to protest about or overcome the obstacles that impede their path. It should not be too difficult for the dreamer to relate such a conflict to her real situation in waking life. The dream says that she is trying to push ahead but keeps slipping back all the time.

Discussion of these interpretations elicited from the dreamer the following opinion: 'I agree about the struggle I am having with myself.'

She also pointed out: 'I do not feel that I am as involved with my daughter as many mothers are, but I do feel involved with my son. Perhaps the sex of offspring wouldn't show up in a dream.'

We can agree with her that this is possible. Just as she

has substituted her sister's child for her own child, so she
may well have substituted one of her children for the
other. In this way the dream succeeds in preserving the
disguise imposed by her conscience on the expression of
her wishes.

'I appreciate your kindness and help with my dreams',
she went on. 'I am struggling with the problem of
understanding myself in order to adjust myself to life's
ups and downs, but I seem to have a pattern of anxiety
and feelings of failure to overcome. I am hoping that in
my dreams I may find a clue to setting about the task.'

This last admission expresses three emotions which
are quite typical of persons who seek self-understanding
through their dreams. The emotions are: gratitude,
puzzlement, and hopefulness. They are hopeful that a
study of their dreams will reveal the underlying
dynamics of their emotional problems. If this study is
pursued far enough, it can be relied upon to fulfil this
hope. They are genuinely bewildered by emotions which
they do not understand and over which they seem to
have no control. It is only in the course of time that they
come to realize that understanding can bring control. To
gain a better knowledge of themselves puts them in a
stronger position to do something about changing their
emotional patterns. Finally, they are grateful, and often
profoundly and touchingly so, to anyone who can show
them a glimmer of light in their confusion. The insight
which the interpretation of a dream can afford them is an
enlightening experience, and they are deeply thankful for
the sense of relief and the lifting of a burden which come
as a result of it.

Let us also hope that many more people will take the
trouble to acquaint themselves with the basic principles
of dream interpretation. Then, when the need arises,
they can act as a source of comfort and illumination to
some fellow human being who is shouldering a heavy
cross of emotional troubles.

INDEX